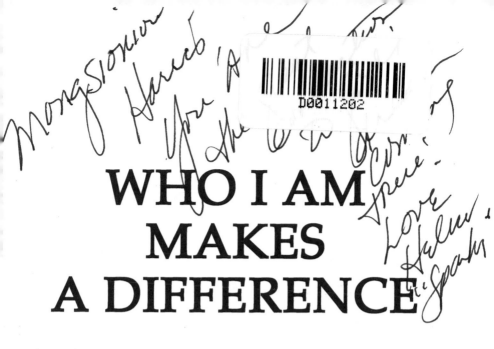

WHO I AM
MAKES
A DIFFERENCE

Stories that Connect People
Heart-to-Heart and
Ignite the Human Spirit

Helice Bridges
First Lady of Acknowledgement

Difference Makers
INTERNATIONAL
Del Mar, California

a non-profit educational foundation
*Creating a world where everyone knows that
who they are makes a difference*

Publisher: Difference Makers International
                    Post Office Box 2115
                    Del Mar, California 92014

Ray Adler, C.E.O.
Book layout and typesetting by Douglas Dunn
Chief Editor and V.P. of Creative Development, Pat Farrell
Photo on cover: Copyright © Alan Hack
Special graphics by Autumn Lew
Cover illustration and design by David Lynch

ISBN 0-9660686-0-2 Trade Paper

Dedication

*To my mom and dad
whose love and support
created a strong foundation
for me to believe in myself and go for my dreams.*

*To my sons
Jay and Marc
for giving me the opportunity to be a mom.
I love you very much.*

*And to the
Difference Makers —
people like yourself
who are taking positive action
to create a world where
everyone knows that
Who They Are Makes a Difference!*

Contents

Acknowledgements

The *Who I Am Makes a Difference* dream was conceived 17 years ago. Nothing great is ever done alone. So many times, over those years, I have felt that the vision was too big for me and I wanted to give up. So many times I thought I should go back to getting a *real job.* But, it was because of all your love and support that I was able to keep going no matter what. In looking back over all these years, every step of the way was a true labor of cocreation, devotion, tears, laughter and full out fun. You gave your hearts and souls to bring this vision into reality. It is a privilege to acknowledge the following people for their dedication and contributions, without which this vision could not be launched and this book would never have been created:

Richard Jardin for being family to me — listening, nurturing, supporting and encouraging me every step of the way for the past 17 years. Your patience and love will forever remain in my heart.

Robert and Susan Roth, my brother and sister-in-law, for being so generous, helping me out over the years, lovingly caring for our mom, and sharing your deep appreciation for my work.

The Hunger Project, under the direction of Joan Holmes, for the opportunity to Co-chair the San Diego Chapter with my partner, Rex Paris. This experience gave me the idea to end the starvation for acknowledgement.

Diana Loomans, my dear friend, enlightened genius and author of many best selling books, for guiding me to believe in myself. Thank you for telling me that I *was* an author, years before I had any stories in print.

Brad Creer, my top cheerleader, for constantly encouraging me over these past 10 years to keep on keeping on.

Barbara Curl, for teaching me how to see my vision clearly and know I could do it!

Senator John Vasconcellos, for pioneering the California Task Force for Self-Esteem and Personal and Social Responsibility. Thank you for sending me a note in 1987 telling me to keep passing out those Blue Ribbons and cheering people on. Even though you didn't know me personally, you were aware of my work and took the time to write. I received your letter at a time when I was ready to give up. Your letter kept me going.

Sanford Goodkin, Brad Creer, Mike Garrett, Lauri Vogel Kittredge, Darryl Wigfall and Pat Yeiser for being our first Board of Directors through the early days and continuously helping me to stay with my vision.

Mark Victor Hansen and Jack Canfield, co-authors of the *Chicken Soup for the Soul* series, for continuously coaching, encouraging me and creating an avenue, through your books, for the *Who I Am Makes a Difference* message to gain world-wide attention. It was your dream that the contributors to your books would expand their careers and further their self-expression in the world. We are people of many words, yet there are no words to express my gratitude for your vision of *Chicken Soup for the Soul.*

Dr. Robert Dobrin, for looking me straight in the eyes in June, 1996, in a no-fooling around way exclaiming, "You must write your book now!"

Marcia Snow, for your great cheer leading, enthusiasm and loving insistence that I get a book published immediately so you could get me on a speaking tour throughout the world. Your enthusiasm and belief in my work gave me the final push to get started right away.

Pat Farrell, V.P. of Training and Development for Difference Makers International, for being a fearless lady, extraordinary mom and someone who *always* goes for it! Thank you for saying *"yes!"* to everything that's needed. You not only headed up the editing team, opened your home for weekly editing meetings, but also served everyone a piping hot dinner every time they showed up!

To the editing team: Michael Citrin, Joe Connor, Sean Kochis, Christina Rathbun, Valerie Rynning and

Marcia Snow for your enlightened presence every week for over three months, gifting your time, energy and unconditional love. You all worked side-by-side, continuously laughing, playing and validating one another while simultaneously digging deep into each story, changing and re-arranging my words. A special thanks to John Sullivan, who came to my home one afternoon just to say hello and wound up agreeing to re-read all the edited stories and make needed corrections. Deborah Brown, thanks for laughing, crying, being on time and devoting so much time to the final edit.

I also want to thank the following people who read the first, very rough draft, helped me make final selections, and gave invaluable comments to help improve my writing and the book cover: Lynn Adams, Melissa Akers, Alan Collier, Arian, Michael Citrin, Marsha Collins, Joe Connor, Dominic D'Arcy, Dr. Robert Dobrin, Pat Farrell, Ken Foster, Alan Hack, Deni Harris, Lisa Kalison, Jeff Kahn, Diana Loomans, Carmita Magee, Sydney Murray, Janet Painter, Harley Rynning, Valerie Rynning, and Marcia Snow. Special thanks to Cheri Diamond for transcribing all the stories and Laura Hill, Jim Rice and Heidi Mercill for jumping in at the last minute and editing the final copy.

Ray Adler, C.E.O. of Difference Makers International for being an inspirational leader, authentic human being and a person who represents my vision at the highest level. Thank you for taking over *all* the business details so that I could finally become the author, speaker and trainer that I have forever longed to be.

Bert Carder and Susie Fields, for being one of the most exuberant and enlightened husband and wife teams on the planet. Thanks for taking me step-by-step through the process of self-publishing this book.

Nancy Schlieser, for being my former assistant. You organized all my files, sales desk, made me laugh all the time, designed and hand made my birthday invitations, fixed the computer, and put the picture on my bathroom mirror that says, *"Helice — you're the top banana!"*

Morgen Espe for cheering me on throughout the day, assisting me, answering the phones, taking orders and bringing me large glasses of water and reminding me to drink it!

Heidi Mercill, for taking charge of packaging and shipping of all our Blue Ribbon products with integrity and beauty. I was ever so grateful the day you walked into my office, looked at the shipping department, and without a word, took it over completely. You found the perfect size boxes, glorious blue tissue and gold seals for the finishing touch. That's a long way from the little brown envelopes I used to send everything out in.

A special thank you to my "hand-selected team" who answered my call in January, 1996, traveled to the Disneyland Hotel in Anaheim, California and laid a foundation which would eventually insure that the *Who I Am Makes a Difference* message would reach 265 million Americans by the year 2000 — with no one left out! Those present were: Kathleen Osta, our master facilitator, Lynn Adams, Bert Carder, Brad Creer, Chip Eichelberger, Pat Farrell, Susie Fields, Jim Hess, Elizabeth Grow, Roberta Mack, Brett Perlmutter, Kathryn Smithen, Denise Wright and Pat Yeiser.

Blessings go to DMI's Board of Directors: Helice Bridges — Chair, Elizabeth Grow, Brett Perlmutter, Michael Price, Kathryn Smithen, Marcia Snow and Denise Wright. What an aligned team! Every company in the world would wish for a Board like ours. Elizabeth, our divine, graceful and playful mind/body coach is a model for inner and outer beauty. Thank you for providing the processes that teach the members of our Board how to stay centered, balanced and in the eye of God. Brett, you are a wizard at combining bottom-line with heartfelt direction. Thank you for hanging in there with me and continually coaching me how to recognize how valuable the *Who I Am Makes a Difference* message is. Michael, for your high level of consciousness, business genius, and generosity. Thank you for loaning me your dictating machine to tape the stories in this book, and opening your magnificent home for our initial editing and book cover meetings. Kathryn, for being a soft, loving and tenacious woman who absolutely never gives up getting what she wants. Marcia, for always having a smile on your face, love in your heart, and commitment in your soul. Denise, for your enthusiasm, hysterical humor and determination to gain strategic alliances with major corporations.

I'm forever grateful to the following team of health professionals and coaches for keeping me healthy, happy and functioning at maximum capacity. Drs. David and Lori Libs, for seeing my vision and gifting me 12 years of chiropractic adjustments so that I could stay in top shape to pursue my vision. Dr. Richard Kaye, for your present of hundreds of Network Chiropractic adjustments which released *all* my stress and gave me the energy to easily accomplish all my work. Alan Collier, for being my inner tennis coach, laughing with me and teaching me how to love that little green ball. Elizabeth Grow, for gifting me Hellerwork sessions. Your deep tissue work released years of pent up emotion, grounded me and lengthened my spine! Jonathan Simmons for being my personal trainer at Frogs Gym and *never* allowing me to stop, even when I thought I couldn't do one more lunge. Ralph White, for being an incredible business coach. The past two years you spent an hour every week teaching me how to be way out in front of what was needed. I now know that *everything* is possible because of your direction and understanding.

Special thanks to some of my teachers, trainers and role models: Werner Erhard, the creator of *est*, who showed me how to create a world that worked for everyone. Robert Fritz, the creator of "Technologies for Creating," who taught me how to move from where I am to where I want to be. Patricia McDade, the creator and trainer of "The Entrepreneurial Edge." I describe you as a cross between a Mother Teresa and a Ted Turner. By your profound example, you have shown me the "way" to make *every* dream I have a reality.

Paul & Layne Cutright, for giving me a bridge from being co-dependent to discovering the type of loving relationship I deserve. Robert Allen, for gifting me business trainings, hosting brainstorming meetings at your home and telling me that I was creating *a miracle in a moment*. Harv Eker, for contributing your business trainings and your wisdom. Deni Harris, for modeling business leadership with heart. Kathleen Osta, for flying out to California on your own dime and dollar, and facilitating our 3-day meeting at the Disneyland Hotel. Don Wolfe, for being a colleague, a friend and for hypnotizing me so that I could see my vision clearly and communicate it to others.

Peter Meisen, President of Global Energy Network International, for being one of the most courageous visionaries on the planet today.

Alvin Morrison for being so generous — designing and presenting us with an extraordinary logo for all the world to see.

Douglas Dunn, for your typesetting skills, your determination to get the book completed on time, and your kindness to do so much more than we originally discussed. Thank you, Doug. We couldn't have done it without you.

Patrick D'Acre for volunteering to be the stage manager for my musical "Shaking Hands with Destiny." You worked your tail off at both performances, arriving hours before anyone else and being the last to leave. You handled the lights, music, and timing of every performer. Your work was impeccable. And when the performance was over, and everyone was gone, you and I sat down in the quiet auditorium. You told me to sit silently and look at the stage. I did. And then in a soft whisper, you asked me recall the spotlight on the stage and to remember what had happened that evening and the difference it had made.

Chandra Schwartz, for being an amazingly talented young lady. Thank for debuting my song, at the age of 14, and getting a standing ovation. You not only have a world-class voice, but an inner and outer beauty that continuously makes a difference in my life!

Jean Farrell for your generous contribution which made it possible to purchase 50,000 Blue Ribbons for children in 20 San Diego elementary, junior and senior high schools during Blue Ribbon Week, proclaimed by Mayor Susan Golding.

Special thanks for beyond the call of duty goes to: Richard Alan, for believing in my Broadway musical. Allana Alexander, for being my exquisite hair dresser and gifting me years of cuts and coloring so that I would *always* look beautiful. Angela Aschbrenner, for believing in me from the very first moment we met. Bill & Donna Bardallis, for working with me to create a corporate sponsorship program for schools. Deborah Beagler, for loaning me your clothes, credit card and constant support at a time when I was very fragile. Jim Benson, for designing our Blue Ribbon Package. Mary Bixby, for your on-going cheer leading and belief in me. Fran Cannon for creating Dream Weavers and spreading the message of acknowledgement to 10,000 people.

Robin Blanc, for being a great friend and one of the best networkers on the planet. Jim and Dana Blessing, for making your dreams come true. Devon Blaine for your generosity, sincerity and great direction in the area of public relations. Lori Bloom, for the year of massages you generously contributed to me. Rayana Blackwell, for establishing Difference Makers International in Vancouver, Canada. Joyce Chapman, for reminding me that I could do it when everyone else said I was crazy. Chris & Carolyn Chase, for being both incredible humanitarians as well as outstanding role models for building teams that easily and effectively produce your Earth Day events with 50,000 people or more. Bobbi DePorter, for cocreating "SuperCamp" and being a great model of a woman owned business that makes a global difference. Stephanie Davis, for offering me the use of your office, computer and assisting me at every turn of the way.

Stephen Longfellow Fiske, for co-writing the lyrics and writing the *Who I Am Makes a Difference* music which was played on ABC's 20/20. Keith Heldman, for co-writing the music and words to *There's a Place Inside of Us All*. Tom Howard, for your brilliant and original writing for the lyrics and music to "You're My Shining Star," and allowing me to use it at my musical debut at the Lyceum Theater in San Diego. Scott Kalechstein for helping me compose the song, "Get With It," for my musical debut at the Lyceum Theater. Floyd Geis, for helping me with my first business plan. Carol Goldstein, for your commitment to teaching *Technologies for Creating* and continuously using the Blue Ribbons to acknowledge all your students. Fern Gorin, for getting your Masters, creating your own company, living your dream and teaching others how to do the same. Phil & Leota Heathman, for feeding me home cooking, giving me a place to sleep and loving me.

Ruth Hirth, for printing the Blue Ribbons for the first 14 years and *always* extending me credit so that I didn't have to come up with the payment right away.

Eric Jensen, for cocreating "SuperCamp" and demonstrating that a person can spend his life surfing and making a global difference. Dermon Lewis, for being a dedicated father, and a man destined to make a positive impact on the lives of thousands. Jill Lublin, for supporting me as a key-note presenter and for your creative ideas in public relations.

Autumn Lew, for being the most brilliant, talented and fun-to-work with graphics designer. Jill McManigal, for looking gorgeous, being a great school teacher and graciously contributing your time toward directing our musical chorus line so that we were as precision as the Rockettes. Jobi Mindell, for being a long-time friend and supporter in the early days when I did not know who I was or where I was going. Dee Parrish, for volunteering to continuously run all over town for me, doing errands.

Gary Oelze, for saying that I was an author and buying me my first computer to prove it. Thanks a million for being my friend all these years and trusting that I would make it. Russ Phelps, for taking your time to help me run my ideas past you for your expert input. Thanks again for leading me down the path at Torrey Pines State Beach and connecting my soul to God. Carol Pugmire, for being such an outstanding model for progressive education and so much fun to have lunch with. Jane Randall, for assisting me and leaving me notes of acknowledgement on every wall of my house. Peter Reding, for giving our team a spiritual insight into producing our business plan and knowing us so well. Valerie Rynning for bringing organization into the office and for orchestrating my 55th birthday party with incredible success.

Lisa Roth, for making me laugh, helping me out at my first musical presentation and for being the greatest niece an aunt could have. Marianna Seward, for generously opening up your heart and your rolodex and connecting us with people who could help us. Jan Newman-Seligman, for the generosity and guidance you extended to me during stressful periods. Randy Smith, for showing up at almost every meeting I had in the early days and believing in me. Cathy, Daniel and James Schmachtenberger, for supporting me, making the chorus line hats and doing everything possible to continuously spread the Blue Ribbon message. Millie Shea, for volunteering at my home every week and being a model for how a 70 year old woman can play golf, travel and keep taking classes to raise her self-esteem.

Carol Star, for making it possible for me to get to the Soviet Union and produce the Blue Ribbon Certificates. Dale & Mark Steele, for taking a stand for my dream and introducing me to the President of Jack-in-the-Box. Christopher Stone, for recording all the music for my musical and showing me that I *could* sing. Sharon Terrill, for telling me that I was a fledgling and choosing to help me fund my first school program. John Thickstun, for being a great attorney and co-signing a loan that made it possible for me to fly to Hawaii and do my first key-note speech. Sandra Thorpe, for being an incredible visionary, making your dream come true for children and making certain that I enrolled in The Entrepreneurial Edge. Ben Tulao, for your integrity, hard work, design and production of our T-shirts, getting my car painted and fixed up for only a little bit of money, and just being a man of a million talents.

Yves Vincent, for generously opening up your music studio to me where we were able to record my song and audio cassette tapes. Dave & Doretta Winkleman, for being outstanding networkers and for believing in me. Karen Wilkening, for loaning me the use of your computer whenever I needed it. Mark Yeeles, for making it possible for me to debut my musical at the prestigious Lyceum Theater in Downtown San Diego and to key-note the Miss Teen America contest. Zannah, for designing the most beautiful greeting cards and including the *Who I Am Makes a Difference* Blue Ribbons. Karen Zarin, for never giving up and making it possible for me to do a school program in Marrietta, Georgia.

Phil Adler for providing our team with spiritual direction. Joe Aguayo for giving us a road map to ensure that our Board of Directors operates at the highest level. Judy Enns for your kindness and unending commitment to our vision.

To the First Blue Ribbon Academy, the greatest team of speakers, trainers, authors, teachers and business professionals: Lynn Adams, Ray Adler, Allana Alexander, Fred Bersche, Dick Caldwell, Bert Carder, Paul & Layne Cutright, Bonnie Dean, Dr. Robert Dobrin, Chip Eichelberger, Harv Eker, Pat Farrell, Elizabeth Grow, Nanci Hartland, Sandi Howlett, Rita Kahn, Ken Kerr, Irene & Sean Kochis, Janay Kruger, Brett Permutter, Chandra Schwartz, Abby Shields,

Kathryn Smithen, Don Wolfe and Denise Wright. Each of you stuck by me while I stumbled over teaching you the first corporate training. Following that two-day training, your direct and unconditional, loving feedback helped me to discover what worked and what needed to be improved. I am forever grateful for your support. Behind the scene, Pat Farrell, your daughter Irene and your son, Sean for working day and night to get everything ready for this training. Cindy Simunec, thanks for your support and ideas that helped launch this training.

Cyndi Farrar, Barbara Goodman and Diana Loomans for being my master mind partners for the last two years. We've surely come a long way with one another's help. Thank you for your depth, directness, vulnerability and willingness to live in the world of possibility.

David Lynch, for designing the cover of this book within only a few days. You masterfully worked with Pat and me and saw our vision immediately.

Because of the enormity of this project, I may have left out the names of some people who helped me along the way. If so, I am sorry — please know that I really do appreciate each of you.

And finally, I am grateful to the living spirit that entrusted me with a vision for a world in which everyone knows that... *Who they are makes a difference.*

About the picture on the front cover

During the eight months it took to complete this book, I looked everywhere for what the cover needed to represent: heart-to-heart connection, love, enthusiasm for life, cocreation and God. Then the day we *had* to make a choice...there it was...right in front of me on the wall of my home — a photo taken by my friend, Alan Hack. I instantly knew that *was* the picture and I had to get in touch with Alan immediately.

In asking Alan's permission, I discovered he had planned to use this very same photo on the cover of his own book. He explained how very important and significant this picture was to him. He took in a deep breath, sat back and thought for a few minutes. A short time later, and consistent with the spirit of the way this entire book has originated, Alan generously and in complete alignment of our collective vision, gifted his photo to us.

You now have the privilege of experiencing this incredible piece of photographic work. Alan is a master of acknowledgement, encouragement and support. He believes in the human spirit and is dedicated to inspiring others to embrace and express their magnificence. Thank you, my friend.

Alan can be reached at:
5580 LaJolla Blvd., #128
LaJolla, California 92037
(619) 491-2573

Introduction

Christopher Columbus saw a vision of a round world, when others only knew it to be flat. I see a vision of a world where anger, apathy and violence are replaced with dignity and respect for all people... **with no one left out!** *There are Difference Makers all over the world supporting this vision. Thank you for being one of them.*
—Helice Bridges, The First Lady of Acknowledgement

In 1983, after having acknowledged over thirty-five thousand people and presenting each with a *Who I Am Makes a Difference* Blue Ribbon, I observed three things: 1. that acknowledgement was missing in our society; 2. that when people received acknowledgement, their physical, social and emotional lives significantly improved; and 3. that when people were healthy, creative and confident — so were others around them.

I remember, as a young girl, the excitement and vitality that Americans had when President John F. Kennedy pointed to the heavens and declared that there would be a man on the moon by the end of the decade. Nine years later, I sat glued to the television and listened intently while Neil Armstrong proclaimed..."*one small step for man, one giant leap for mankind.*"

The TV announcer told us that thousands of people had worked together to make that dream come true. And from that moment on, I knew that, somehow, *everything* was possible!

Although I was only eighteen years old at the time President Kennedy made his declaration, I, too, had a dream — a world where no one was put down and everybody knew they made a difference. When I told people my dream, they laughed at me and said it was impossible. Nevertheless, something deep inside kept telling me that together we could also make this dream come true.

For thirty-seven years I have held this vision. I imagined a world in which 5.5 billion people on our planet were modeling the language of acknowledgement. I imagined acknowledgement at the core of every communication. I imagined young and old, men and women, people of every race, religion, and economic status working together to create a global environment where dignity and respect for all people replace anger, apathy and violence. I imagined that *you* were one of those people who contributed to making this dream come true.

In 1984, I finally discovered the steps to teach others how to recreate my acknowledgement process. I wrote these steps down and called it *The Blue Ribbon Ceremony.*

I was now ready (or so I thought) to write a little book explaining the power of *The Blue Ribbon Ceremony.* The book would be filled with short stories about people whose lives had significantly changed for the better after having been acknowledged. Inside each book would be my gift of ten *magic* Blue Ribbons so that everyone would have a hands-on tool to immediately "walk the acknowledgement talk."

I was on fire with excitement to complete the book quickly, print it and have it ready within one month. I knew in my heart that this compact little book would be in everyone's briefcase, purse or pocket. People in corporations, organizations, schools, churches, homes and neighborhoods would use the Blue Ribbon as a tool to cultivate authentic communication, bring out the best in everyone and bring smiles, hugs and cheers to every corner of the globe. I could feel, taste, touch and see this as absolute.

In July, 1988, I completed the book and produced a musical celebration, all within eleven days. I turned the manuscript over to a volunteer who did all the transcribing. From there I took it directly to the printer. During those eleven days, I raised enough money to print seventeen hundred books. Each book contained a small envelope with ten Blue Ribbons and the *Blue Ribbon Ceremony.*

The musical was developing and everything was on schedule. Tickets were sold and approximately 150 people were expected to fill the small theater. All was a go.

The morning before the kick-off, I picked up seventeen hundred books from the printer and carefully glued a gold seal on each one (best selling books have gold seals!). That evening, my Board of Directors anxiously awaited the unveiling of my book.

Like a small child opening presents on Christmas morning, I opened the box and pulled out enough books to pass around to all twelve members of the Board. I anticipated them holding those sweet little books in their hands, approving of the title *The Spirit of Excellence* and the dedication: *That every child shall grow up in a safe, supportive, nurturing environment in which they will always know that Who They Are Makes a Difference and that dreams really do come true.*

I waited for them to say…"What a wonderful title!" "Good work!" "Great job!" Instead, they sat in stone silence. Then, gradually, one-by-one they announced, "Helice, there's a spelling mistake on the back cover, and three errors on page 2, another on page 6…" In fact, they found one hundred and sixty errors in my little 52 page book. In addition, page 52 was upside-down and backwards and was really page 18.

"You can't give out this book tomorrow night!" they exclaimed in unison.

"Doesn't anybody see what I've done right?" I cried. "What about the vision for children, and the envelope of Blue Ribbons? Isn't that a good idea? And look, after acknowledging thirty-five thousand people, *The Blue Ribbon Ceremony* is finally in print. That's a monumental accomplishment! Why don't you forget the spelling errors for a moment and simply concentrate on the stories? They prove that the power of acknowledgement actually transforms people's lives in only a minute or less. We must give out this book tomorrow night!" I insisted.

"Helice," the Chair of the Board announced, "this book is entitled *The Spirit of Excellence* and this book is *not* excellent. People will read this book and think that it's a joke. They will *only* see your spelling errors. You must *never* give out any of these books!"

And that was their final word. I left the meeting broken hearted. Why couldn't they have applauded my effort? Couldn't they see that the vision was so much more important than the spelling errors? Why couldn't I just explain that I was not a very good speller and ask them to look past my mistakes? What's so wrong with that?

With that idea in mind, I spent the rest of the night writing a note on page 52 which said, "This is really page 18. Please excuse the error. Love, Helice."

The next evening, despite the direction of my Board, I handed out 150 books, announced my dedication to the children and expressed my apologies for the spelling errors. Although the musical celebration was a success, my Board was livid and severely chastised me. Feeling lost and alone, I returned home that evening and tossed 1,500 books into the trash, leaving only 50 for posterity.

Two weeks later, I received a surprising call from Joyce Fuller and Audrey Eicher, special education teachers in the Boulder Valley School District in Boulder, Colorado. "Jerry Jampolsky, an international lecturer who just spoke to our group, presented us with your Blue Ribbons," said the teacher. "I'd like to know more about them. Could you send me some information?"

"Well, I only have a little book. It costs $10.00 and comes with ten Blue Ribbons. I'm not supposed to send it to you because it contains a great many spelling errors. But if you don't look at the spelling mistakes and just look at my vision, I will send a copy to you." And that is what I did. Within a month after the school teacher ordered the book, the Colorado School District sent me $30 for three more books. They had read my book, saw only my vision and wrote a grant to order three thousand more Blue Ribbons.

I wish that I could tell you that the order from the Colorado School District inspired me to re-write the book immediately. But it didn't. I tried, but nobody wanted to help me. I was crushed, shut down, and afraid to write again. My self-esteem plummeted to zero. For the next eight years, I was frozen, uncreative and constantly fearful that anything I would do would be filled with mistakes.

It took me almost nine years before I put my stories into a written form. This is the book you are now reading, a book developed far differently than my first one.

No, my spelling has not gotten any better, but my self-esteem has. The first little book taught me five very important lessons: 1. that pointing out faults and fail-ures shuts down and destroys the human spirit; 2. that risk taking and mistakes are a necessary backbone of creativity and genius; 3. that acknowledgement is a basic human need which propels *all* people toward their highest vision of themselves and humanity; 4. that nothing great is ever done alone; and 5. that acknowledgement bridges the gap between young and old, men and women — people of every race, religion, and economic status.

The first book was written by myself. This one is not. Every step of the way there was generous support from my friends and colleagues. They contributed their time and energy to helping me edit, compose and compile this book. Most importantly, through-out the process, each one constantly acknowledged the contributions of the others. No one focused on the mistakes or faults of anyone, but rather gifted their unique talents. Love and acknowledgement is woven into every fiber of this book. It is our gift to you and one that you rightly deserve.

This book is no longer the dream of one person, for acknowledgement belongs to everyone. The moment you acknowledge another person with the Blue Ribbon, you become part of an international team of people known as *Difference Makers* — pioneers who are spearheading the language of acknowledgement for the new millennium. As a *Difference Maker,* you can now share in the dream. Enclosed is my special gift to you of six *Who I Am Makes a Difference* Blue Ribbons. Decide today to acknowledge someone. Begin with your children, spouse, parent, boss, colleague or neighbor. Acknowledge them now! And know that every time you stop to tell a person that they matter — they do. Thank you from the bottom of my heart. ***Who You Are Makes A Difference!***

Dear God,

So far today, God, I've done alright. I haven't lost my temper, haven't been greedy, grumpy, nasty, selfish or over-indulgent. I'm really glad about that.

But in a few minutes, God, I'm going to get out of bed and from then on I'm probably going to need a lot more help.

Thank you,

Amen

—unknown

1

Who I Am Makes A Difference

Do all things with love.

—Og Mandino

A teacher in New York decided to honor all of her high school seniors by telling each of them how much of a difference they made. Using the *Who I Am Makes a Difference* Ceremony, she called each student to the front of the class, one at a time. First she told the class how that student made a difference to her. Then, she presented each of them with a *Who I Am Makes a Difference* Blue Ribbon.

Afterwards the teacher decided to do a class project to see what kind of impact acknowledgement would have on their community. She gave each of the students three more ribbons and instructed them to go out and spread this Blue Ribbon Ceremony. They were to follow up on the results, see who honored whom and report back to the class in about a week.

One of the boys in the class went to a junior executive in a nearby company and honored him for having helped him with his career planning. The boy gave him a Blue Ribbon, placing it on his shirt just above his heart. Then he gave the junior executive two extra ribbons, and said, "We're doing a class project on acknowledgement, and we'd like you to go out and find someone to honor. Give them this Blue Ribbon, then give them the extra Blue Ribbon so they can acknowledge another person to keep this acknowledgement ceremony going. Then, please report back to me and tell me what happened."

Later that day the junior executive went in to see his boss, who had been noted, by the way, as being kind of a grouchy fellow. He sat his boss down and told him that he deeply admired him for being a creative genius. The junior executive asked him if he would accept the gift of the Blue Ribbon and would he give him permission to put it on him. His surprised boss said, "Well, sure."

The junior executive took the Blue Ribbon and placed it right on his boss' jacket above his heart. As he gave him the last extra ribbon, he said, "Would you do me a favor? Would you take this extra ribbon and pass it on by honoring someone else? The young boy who first gave me the ribbons is doing a project in school and we want to keep this recognition ceremony going to find out how it affects people."

That night the boss went home to his 14-year-old son and sat him down. He said, "The most incredible thing happened to me today. I was in my office and one of the junior executives came in and told me he admired me and gave me a Blue Ribbon for being a creative genius. Imagine. He thinks I'm a creative genius. Then he put this Blue Ribbon that says *Who I Am Makes a Difference* on my jacket above my heart. He gave me an extra ribbon and asked me to find someone else to honor. As I was driving home tonight, I started thinking about whom I would honor with this ribbon and I thought about you. I want to honor you.

"My days are really hectic and when I come home I don't pay a lot of attention to you. Sometimes I scream at you for not getting good enough grades in school or for your bedroom being a mess. But somehow tonight, I just wanted to sit here and, well, just let you know that you *do* make a difference to me. Besides your mother, you are the most important person in my life. You're a great kid and I love you!"

The startled boy started to sob and sob. He couldn't stop crying. His whole body shook. He looked up at his father and said through his tears, "I was planning on committing suicide tomorrow, Dad, because I didn't think you loved me. Now I don't need to."

School teacher
Rochester, New York — 1988

Since this story appeared in Chicken Soup for the Soul, we have received calls from around the world, resulting in 25,000 people a month now being acknowledged.

YES! Imagine A World ...

Imagine

Imagine

... Imagine ... Imagine

Imagine a world where each of us is recognized as a special creation with unique qualities and capabilities. *Imagine a world* where everyone is truly appreciated and found valuable to society. *Imagine a world* where the special gifts of children are encouraged and nurtured by the adults who spend time with them. *Imagine a world* where the consciousness supports freedom of choice and awareness of responsibility. *Imagine a world* where everyone is encouraged to express their particular talents in an environment of creativity, enthusiasm, support, exploration, cooperation and safety. *Imagine a world* where we relate to one another with love, trust and acceptance of individual differences. *Imagine a world* where it is openly acknowledged that "yes! we are all extra special" and deserve to treat ourselves and everyone with honor and respect.

YES! Imagine this kind of world into reality.

28

2

The Blind Man

Most of us remain strangers to ourselves, hiding who we are, and ask other strangers, hiding who they are, to love us.
— Leo Buscaglia

Buses, trains, airplanes and airports offer a safe haven for strangers to divulge intimate stories, knowing that they will probably never see one another again. Such was the case one day in the spring of 1983 at La Guardia Airport. I was waiting for my plane when a tall, strong, handsomely tailored gentleman felt safe enough in his anonymity to sit next to me and share the following story:

"I was finishing up my work at my office in downtown Manhattan. My secretary had left about a half hour before. I was just getting ready to pack up for the day when the phone rang. It was Ruth, my secretary. She was in a panic. 'I've left an important package on my desk by mistake. It needs to be delivered immediately to the Blind Institute. It's only a few blocks away. Could you please help me out?'

" 'You caught me at a good time. I was just walking out the door. Sure. I'll drop the package off for you.'

"As I walked into the Blind Institute, a man ran toward me. 'Thank heaven you've arrived. We must get started at once.' He pointed to an empty chair next to him and told me to sit down. Before I could say anything, I was sitting in a row of people who were all sighted. Directly facing us was a row of sightless men and women. A young man, about 25 years old, stood in front of the room. He began giving us instructions.

" 'In a moment, I will ask those of you who are sightless to get to know the person seated across from you. It will be important for you to take whatever time you need to distinguish their features, hair texture, bone type, rate of breathing and so forth. When I say 'begin', you will reach across and touch the person's head, feel the texture of their hair, note if it is curly or straight, coarse or thin. Imagine what color it might be. Then slowly place your fingers on their brow. Feel the strength, the size, the texture of the skin. Use both hands to investigate their eyebrows, eyes, nose, cheeks, lips, chin and neck. Listen to the person's breathing. Is it calm or rapid? Can you hear their heart beating? Is it fast or slow? Take your time. Now, begin.'

"I began to panic. I wanted out of this place. I don't allow anybody to touch me without my permission, let alone a man. I remember thinking, 'He's touching my hair. God, this is uncomfortable. Now his hands are on my face. I'm perspiring. He'll hear my heart beating and know I'm panicking. Got to calm down. Can't show him that I'm not in control.' I felt a sign of relief when it was finally over.

"The young instructor continued, 'Now the sighted people will have the same opportunity to discover the person seated across from them. Close your eyes and imagine that you have never seen this person in your life. Decide what you want to know about this person. Who are they? What are their thoughts? What kind of dreams might they have? Reach across and begin to touch their head. Feel the texture of their hair. What color is their hair?'

"His voice faded into the background. Before I could stop, I had my hands on this young man's head seated across from me. His hair felt dry and coarse. I couldn't remember the color of his hair. I have never remembered the color of anybody's hair.

"In fact, I'd never really looked at anyone. I just told people what to do. People were dispensable to me...I never really cared about them. My business was important. The deals I made were important. This touching, feeling and knowing other people, was definitely not me, nor would it ever be.

"I continued to touch the young man's eyebrows, nose, cheeks and chin. I felt myself weeping inside. There was a tenderness in my heart that I had not known, a vulnerability I had never revealed to myself or anyone else around me. I felt it and was afraid. It was clear to me that when I left this building, I would go and never come back.

"Dreams? Did this young man across from me have dreams? Why should I care? He's nothing to me. I've got two teenage kids and I don't even know their dreams. Besides, all they ever think about is cars, sports and girls. We don't talk much. I don't understand them. I don't even think they like me. My wife...well, she does her thing and I do mine.

"I was perspiring and breathing hard. The instructor told us to stop. I removed my hands from his face and sat back. 'Now,' he went on, 'this is the last part of the exercise. You will each have three minutes to share with each other how you experienced getting to know your partner. Let your partner know what you were thinking and feeling. Tell them what you learned about them. The sightless person will go first.'

"My partner's name was Henry. He told me that, at first, he felt left out because he didn't think he was going to have a partner for the evening. He was glad that I was able to make it on time. He went on to tell me that I was truly courageous to risk feeling my emotions. 'I was impressed,' he explained, 'at the way you followed the instructions despite how resistant you were to them. Your heart is very big and very lonely. You want more love in your life but you don't know how to ask for it. I admire your willingness to discover the side of you that truly makes a difference. I know you wanted to bolt out of this room, but you stayed. I felt the same way when I first came here. But now I'm no longer afraid of who I am. It's okay for me to cry, feel afraid, panic, want to run, shut down from others, or hide out in my work. These are just normal emotions that I am learning to accept and appreciate. You might want to spend more time down here and learn who you really are.'

"I looked across at this young sightless Henry and wept openly. I couldn't speak. There was nothing to say. I had never known a place like this in my entire life. I had never experienced this amount of unconditional love and wisdom. The only thing I remember saying to Henry was, 'Your hair is brown and your eyes are light.' He was probably the first person in my life whose eyes I would never forget. I was the blind man and it was Henry who had the vision to see who I was.

"It was time for the meeting to end. I picked up the envelope under my seat and brought it to the instructor. 'My secretary was supposed to drop this off to you earlier this evening. Sorry it got here late.'

"The instructor smiled and took the package saying, 'This is the first time I have ever run an evening like this. I had been waiting for the instructions to arrive so I would know what to do. When they didn't get here, I just had to wing it. I didn't realize that you weren't one of the regular volunteers. Please accept my apologies.'

"I haven't told anyone, not even my secretary, that I go to the Blind Institute two nights a week now. I can't explain it, but I actually think I'm starting to feel love for people. Don't tell anyone on Wall Street I said that. You know, it's a dog-eat-dog world and I have to stay on top of it...or do I? I don't seem to have answers to anything anymore.

"I know I've got a lot of learning and growing to do if I want my sons to respect me. Funny, I've never said that before. Kids are *supposed* to respect their parents, or at least that's what I've always been told. Maybe it goes both ways. Maybe we can learn how to respect each other. For now, I'm just beginning to learn how to respect and love myself. Imagine what it would be like if we all had the vision to see with our hearts."

Helice — 1982

3

Everyone Is Famous
To Someone

The greatest good is what we do for one another.
— Mother Teresa

In 1992, Rio de Janeiro was the site of the Environmental Earth Summit. Approximately thirty thousand global leaders would be attending. Soon I would be speaking on creating a safe global environment for children along with a gentleman named, Al Gore, and other global leaders.

During that time of my life, my focus was on teaching self-esteem programs and not on the environment. In fact, in those days I didn't even recycle cans! Nonetheless, when I was invited to be a key-note speaker, my friends convinced me that it would be an opportunity of a lifetime and that my Blue Ribbon message was essential for the world to hear.

The Summit began on the twenty-five hour flight from San Diego to Rio. The plane was filled with the vitality of leaders from around the world. There was an electricity in the plane as visionaries greeted one another, exchanged four color brochures and hugged. I wanted desperately to go up to them, shake hands and make their acquaintance. Instead, I sat silently in my seat, afraid to disturb the two Buddhist Monks seated on either side of me who remained deep in meditation during the entire flight. I was elated when the plane finally touched down in Rio.

Standing in the long registration line at the Hotel Gloria, I was once again surrounded by important global figures. CNN cameras were everywhere. My stomach felt queasy. I looked around for a familiar friendly face. I longed for companionship — just anybody that I could speak with. But instead of feeling elated, I was tongue tied and intimidated. I couldn't wait to get to my room, shower and fall into a deep sleep.

By the next morning, I was back to my normal self, ready to go out and meet the world. I took the elevator down to the lobby floor. When the doors opened, I was taken back by what I saw. Only ten feet from me was Shirley MacLaine speaking with Bella Abzug. From the corner of my eye, I saw Olivia Newton John going up the escalator while John Denver was coming down. Simultaneously Jacques Cousteau was pulling up in a white limousine as the Dali Lama stepped into the hotel, surrounded by fifty armed guards. Five CNN camera men raced toward him, bumping into me and smashing me against the wall like a fly.

Everywhere I turned, there was a person I had always wanted to meet. My eye caught the politically outspoken and courageous Bella Abzug, talking with Shirley MacLaine. I had admired Bella from afar for many years and decided that I would take the plunge and boldly walk up to her and present her with a Blue Ribbon.

I waited politely for her to say good-bye to Shirley before I approached her. But before I could blink, she had run outside and hailed a taxi. I panicked and raced after her. I stood two feet in front of her and stood frozen, unable to speak. She was now deeply engrossed in a conversation with a women who appeared to be her publicist. Finally, I took in a deep breath, told myself to just go for it, and interrupted her (very impolite, I know). "Excuse me Bella, I have a Blue Ribbon that says *Who I Am Makes a Difference* and I would like to acknowledge you for making such a significant difference in my life. May I have permission to put this on you?"

She responded as politely as she could under the circumstances. I quickly placed the ribbon over her heart giving her extra ones to give away to others. She turned to her publicity agent and matter-of-factly slapped a ribbon on her without saying a word and jumped into the waiting taxi.

As the cab pulled away, the exhaust from this third world taxi slapped me in the face. I felt like Linus without my blanket. I was on shaky ground. Everyone around me was *so* important. "Who am I?" I asked myself. These people have their faces on the covers of magazines and four color brochures. All I had was a Blue Ribbon.

Devastated, I dragged myself back into the lobby, intent on hiding out in my hotel room for the remainder of the day. The lobby had cleared out and I was thankful for the quiet.

"Excuse me," said a stunning, attractively dressed woman, "I am the hotel manager. I heard that you were the person who acknowledged one of our maids this morning and gave her a Blue Ribbon."

"Yes, I did that," I said.

"Well, it has changed her entire life. She's been running around telling everyone that a very famous person told her that she made a difference. I can't thank you enough. I know that she will never forget this moment."

It was then that I realized that each of us is famous to someone else. I do not need to have my name in the paper, a picture on the front cover of a magazine or a four color brochure to make a difference. All I needed to be was myself, to do everyday that which was my God given nature — to acknowledge those around me and tell them that *Who they are makes a difference!*

Helice Bridges

You

Must

Be The

Change

You

Wish

To See

In

The

World

— *Mahatma Gandhi*

4

An Assembly of Love

I own everything about me — my body...my feelings...my actions...I own all my triumphs and successes, all my failures and mistakes...I am me and I am okay.
— Virgina Satir

Two thousand students sat in the gymnasium facing me. Under the direction of Pat Mitchell, the principal, student council, faculty, P.T.A., clergy and neighborhood service groups teamed together to insure that the Blue Ribbon assembly would be supported by the entire community.

"Who You Are Makes a Difference! I shouted. "Every single one of you is important to this world. Over the past 10 years, I have told thousands of people that they made a difference. Then I gave them this Blue Ribbon. No matter whether they were children, teens or adults, the majority of people told me the same thing. 'You're

the first person who has ever told me that I matter. Everybody tells me what I do wrong. Nobody tells me what I do right.'

"So far as I've been able to tell, everyone thinks that they are the only one who gets harassed and put down. The truth is, it's happening *everywhere* and today, right now, we can begin to change this condition."

"You sir, yes you, seated over there. Would you kindly come up to the stage with me," I said pointing to the boy in the 3rd row.

The students started cheering and clapping as Jerry ran up. I had obviously picked a popular student. "Jerry, I'm presenting this Blue Ribbon to you that says *Who I Am Makes a Difference* because I've had my eye on you ever since I came on the stage. I appreciate the attention you have given me. I have a sense that you are a great leader. Would you accept this gift from me?"

He nodded his head. The audience watched in silence, not really knowing what to think about all of this. Next I presented him with extra Blue Ribbons to give to others. He immediately said he knew who he would give them to. "Can I have a hug?" I asked.

"Sure," he answered, immediately throwing his arms around me. The audience hooted, hollered and applauded as Jerry left the stage.

"The next part of this assembly is yours. In a moment, I will step to the side and give each of you an opportunity to come up to the microphone. The purpose will be three fold: Number one: If you have ever harmed anyone, put them down or hurt them in any way at all, I am inviting you to step forward, state your name, what you did and who you harmed. That person can come up to the stage. You may shake hands, give each other a hug or do whatever is natural, but clean it up and say you're sorry. Number two: If you would like to have more love and understanding, now is your time to come and get it. Come up to the stage and ask for what you want.

"Lastly, if you would like to acknowledge your friends, family or teachers —- now is the time to do it. This is your microphone and your assembly. It will be up to you to create a climate in which every person in this school experiences every day that they are important, respected and successful. It will begin with you discovering how to be in relationship with each other without put downs, but rather with acknowledgement."

There was a long pregnant pause. You could hear a pin drop. Then one of the basketball players stood up and walked up the stairs to the stage. The rest of the audience remained silent in their seats.

"There are a lot of cliques in this school. It seems as though if you're not in some gang, on some team, or in some student club, you're nobody. As for me, I'm sick of it! If the basketball players would start to interact with the gang members, and the gang members with the cheer leaders, and all the students in the different school clubs began talking to one another, then I think we could become the kind of community that can work together toward something truly great. It's not enough for me to just be on a winning basketball team. If I'm going to make it in life, I want to have that kind of team spirit in my school, home and community. It's not that way now, but I believe we can work together and make a change."

There was a thunderous applause. Some students even stood up and applauded. As soon as the basketball player stepped off the stage, the flood gates opened. Hundreds of students stormed to the front of the gymnasium and lined up on the stage for their time at the microphone.

"I always tell everyone that my brother is a liar and a cheat," said Melody. "But I'm the liar. He's not really that way at all. You see, I'm just jealous of him and that's the way I've been getting back. So I want to say, 'I'm sorry, Chuck. Will you forgive me?'"

Chuck, a sophomore at the school, slowly stood up. Every eye watched him as he walked the long distance up to the stage. Chuck stepped toward his sister, stopping just in front of her. There were tears streaming down both of their faces. Then, they reached out and hugged one another. I could hear both of them say, "I'm really sorry I hurt you."

Todd came forward next. "I want to apologize to five of my teachers. You call me a hot shot in class because I cut up a lot. But I'm not a hot shot. You see, my girlfriend committed suicide last year and I'm really mixed up. I haven't been able to talk to anybody about it." Todd's eyes flooded with tears. His body shook. I put my hand gently on his shoulder and whispered in his ear. "Take in a deep breath, you're doing great, now look toward the audience. Todd, what you have to say is *very* important for everyone to hear. Keep on going," I coached.

Todd continued, "But I'm not a hot shot. What you see is who I really am. I just need your love and support."

About twenty kids in the line immediately circled around him, giving him hugs and telling him that they would be there for him. Other students ran up to the stage and joined them.

Monaca was next to step to the microphone. "Every day I come to school and you all make fun of me because of my weight." Pointing to another girl in the audience, Monaca continued, "But you devastate that girl and it's not fair for her to be put down in such a horrible way. Just because we have more weight on our bones than you do, is no reason for us to be called fatso, ugly and to be laughed at. I want you all to apologize to my friend by giving her a standing ovation to show that you're sorry for what you've done. From now on, we only want to hear the good things about us because there are plenty of great things that we do!"

The entire audience simultaneously stood up and faced Mary, giving her a thunderous round of applause. I stepped down off the stage and ran over to her. Frightened, she had turned her back to the audience and was facing the wall. I whispered into her ear, "Mary, I know that you're overwhelmed right now, but the entire student body is trying to say they're sorry. Turn around, face them and accept their love. I'll stand right here beside you. You deserve the respect that you are getting now. Go ahead and turn around, I'm right here."

Mary turned around. The entire audience roared and applauded even louder. She trembled and shook. Dozens of students ran up and embraced her.

One by one the students continued to speak. The more they spoke, the more other students were drawn out of their seats to step into the long line on stage. An hour and a half had already passed and there were still hundreds of students waiting for their turn to speak.

Just as another student had approached the microphone, I was motioned off stage by the principal and other city officials. "We've decided to extend this assembly for another half hour. Let the students know that their lunch hour has been extended. We will keep going as long as we can."

As the last student completed, I stepped to the microphone. "Your principal and city officials have decided to extend this assembly for another half hour. Congratulations!"

Once again, the students stood up and gave a standing ovation. This time they knew that they *all* achieved that success together.

Darryl stepped forward. "You all make fun of me because of my stammer. You point at me and tell me that I'm a 'retard.' But I'm not a 'retard' and I don't want you to call me that anymore. In fact, I'd like you to call me handsome. From now on I want you to come up to me and say, 'Darryl, you're handsome!'"

Shark was next. "I'm in a gang because I get treated with respect. A lot of my friends have died and that hurts. None of us show the hurt because we're supposed to be cool. But I'm really hurting and I wish things were different than they are right now."

The final few minutes of the assembly were left to the *handicapable* students and the school choir. The students demonstrated how to sign the Blue Ribbon Ceremony for the deaf. The choir stepped forward, put their arms around each other and sang the song I wrote with Keith Heldman, entitled, "There's a Place Inside of Us All."

Everywhere I looked, I saw students crying and hugging.

Hundreds of students still remained in the line on stage when the assembly time came to an end. Now they would be going back to their classrooms and presenting one another with Blue Ribbons.

As I wandered down the corridors, peeking into the classrooms, I observed rapt attention, as students continued their apologies or requests. Every once in a while a student would run out of their classroom and give me a big hug. One of them was Darryl. "I've never cried before," he exclaimed, "not even when my favorite grandma died this past year. I *never* show my emotions. But during lunch, a whole bunch of students came up to me and said, 'Darryl, you're handsome!' And for the first time in my entire life, I feel as though I'm important."

Helice Bridges

Dear Helice,

I just wanted to thank you for all that you have done for me. You helped me to open up to myself and others and to realize that all things in life aren't bad. I really believe in what you are doing, and I believe in myself.

In the 17 years I've been alive, I've been an abused child. My real father deserted me when I was just a few days old; my first step father beat me and the rest of my family; my mom's ex-boyfriend always told me I was no good; my grandfather molested me when I was 12 years old; and now, all my new step-father can do is argue and yell at me.

When you came to my school Thursday, you put a light in my life; one that has never been there before. You also made me realize that to live and exist in peace you must first be truthful to yourself and to believe that, no matter what goes wrong, there will always be something right at the end of the tunnel.

> *Love,*
> *Sherri — 12th grade*

Dear Helice,

Your student assembly was scheduled for an hour and a half. After two hours, despite protestations from the students, we reluctantly rang the bell for lunch. It had been a cathartic two hours of revelation for our students. For 120 minutes students lined up at the stage to share their feelings with their peers. Apologies, tears, and cheers were the order of the day. Anticipating potential problems with this form of "testimony" we had arranged for psychologists and counselors in the event of any negative after effects. Interestingly, the experience, despite many tears, proved to be an uplifting one and we received no counselor referrals and just one parent inquiry.

The parent meeting the following evening, attracted a crowd of 450 and was an equally moving experience. It certainly fulfilled our expectations of bringing students, parents and staff together as a family.

I can't say that this program will work at every site. Certainly, it requires the support of the administration and staff to be successful. For those schools committed to communication, this type of program will be a "piece of cake." For schools new to "communication" it will be a challenge — but one that promises to justify and risk that might be involved.

Sincerely yours,
Patrick Mitchell
Dean of Activities

Chula Vista High School
Chula Vista, California
1990

5

Honeymooners in the Deli

Kind words can be short and easy to speak, but their echoes are truly endless.

— Mother Teresa

Rita sat in the deli drinking her coffee. In the booth across from her, an elderly couple was arguing. "Moishe," the woman barked, "you never notice all the nice things I do for you."

"Selma, if you weren't so busy taking care of the children and the grandchildren, maybe you'd notice that I do nice things for you all the time," Moishe responded sharply.

Back and forth the couple continued bickering. It was then that Rita recognized a perfect opportunity for a Blue Ribbon acknowledgement. Approaching their table, she politely said, "Excuse me, but I couldn't help noticing how attractively you both are dressed." Turning to look Moishe squarely in the eyes, Rita said, "Your wife has on such a lovely gray suit with matching hat, shoes and purse. She looks stunning."

Turning to face Selma, Rita continued, "You take such good care of your appearance. Your husband must be very proud to be seen with you. It would be my privilege to honor you with this Blue Ribbon that says *Who I Am Makes a Difference*. From the moment I laid eyes on you, I knew that you were a woman who has always taken pride in herself and how she looks. May I place this Blue Ribbon over your heart where it will always remind you of the difference you make?"

Selma nodded her approval as Rita placed the Blue Ribbon on her. "I shall always cheer you on for your dreams," Rita said, placing her hand gently on her shoulder.

"My dream," said Selma, "is to see my children and grandchildren healthy and happy."

"And I know that the love you are giving them now will insure that your dream will come true," Rita proclaimed.

Handing Selma extra Blue Ribbons, Rita continued, "It is a tradition to give you extra Blue Ribbons to acknowledge others. Perhaps you might want to take a moment and acknowledge your husband right now."

Without hesitating, Selma leaned toward her husband and in a sincere hushed voice said, "Moishe, in all these years I've never told you how much it has meant to me to be treated to lunch everyday. We get all dressed up to go to the deli and I always feel beautiful dressing up for you."

As soon as Selma placed the Blue Ribbon on her husband, Moishe reached out and tenderly held her hands in his and quietly whispered, "Selma, I too have always loved the way you dress up for me. We do make a good looking couple!"

Off in the corner of the deli, a few waitresses looked on in awe. As Rita paid her check, the two waitresses approached her. "That's a fine thing you did for that couple," they exclaimed. "They've been bickering for years. Now look at them, just sitting their gazing into each others eyes like newlyweds. Seems that your Blue Ribbon took all their anger away. Think it would work for our husbands?"

Rita smiled, reached into her purse, pulled out some extra Blue Ribbons and handed them to the waitresses. "Here," she said, "everyone deserves a second honeymoon!"

Rita E. — 1983

6

Mr. Gestapo

*People often ask me, "What is the one most significant thing
you've learned about managing and motivating others?" I
tell them that, without question, it's the concept of "catching
people doing something right."*

— Ken Blanchard

Denise, senior vice-president of sales and marketing
for a large California-based company, fumed as she
took her seat next to me. It was unusual for her to be in
a huff. I had grown to love this woman, with her
spontaneous wit and her willingness to see the best in
everyone. She often acknowledged people with a *Who I
Am Makes a Difference* Blue Ribbon to remind them of
the difference they make. It was out of character for her
to be angry.

"I'm so livid," Denise puffed. "The security guard
over by the door is the rudest man I have ever met. He

asked to see my lunch ticket before he would let me enter the room. As a guest of the keynote speaker, I did not realize I needed a ticket. I pointed to my Building Industry badge, demonstrating that I was entitled to enter all the convention activities. He told me that wasn't good enough. He actually shouted at me, 'No ticket, lady, no food!' Remaining cool, I asked him politely where I should go to get a luncheon ticket, but he wouldn't answer. He even put his arm out in front of me to prevent me from going into the room." Those seated at our table quickly agreed that this two-hundred-fifty pound security guard was Mr. Gestapo.

"I demanded his name and badge number," Denise continued, "and I told him I was going to report his rudeness to his supervisor. "Tough," the security guard retorted, "I'm not going to tell you anything."

"Hearing this, I noted his badge number and stormed past him. I can't believe how angry I am right now. I can usually get along with anyone and try to be a loving person, but this guy is something else. I know, Helice, you have always taught me to see the good in others, but this has got to be the exception!"

"It is good that you told him how you felt," I responded. "I imagine that before this afternoon is over, you will acknowledge him and tell him what he has done to make a difference."

"I was afraid you would say that," Denise grimaced.

The keynote speaker, John Martin, is a leader in the Building Industry Association. Committed to making a difference, he concluded his speech by saying, "In our industry, we often don't show enough empathy for people. It is time to reinvent the future, recognize the value in others, communicate compassionately and make a difference in the lives of everyone. It is important for all of us to let our colleagues, friends and family members know how much they matter to us. I would like to invite my business partner onto the stage to acknowledge him with a Blue Ribbon for the difference he has made in my life."

When John completed the Blue Ribbon Ceremony, the two men hugged. Then he invited me to lead the audience of over two-hundred-fifty building industry leaders in the *Who I Am Makes a Difference* Blue Ribbon Ceremony.

Within a few minutes, I shared with the audience how to acknowledge the person seated next to them. As they turned to one another with the Blue Ribbons, I watched their faces light up. Tears, handshakes and hugs spontaneously filled the room. Men slapped each other on the back saying, "I never thought I could do this acknowledgement thing." "I can't believe so-and-so actually acknowledged me. I didn't think I made that kind of difference to him." "This acknowledgement ceremony is really powerful. We ought to do this everywhere!"

I was pleased to see that someone was even acknowledging the stoic security guard. As soon as the Blue Ribbon was placed above his heart, his face went soft like a puppy dog's.

Curious to meet this man, I walked up to him smiling and said, "Hi, I'm glad to see that you received a Blue Ribbon. You truly are a man who does his job with gusto. I imagine it must be a very challenging position."

"You're right about that, lady. This place is chaotic," said the security guard in frustration. "I don't usually work here, but even I can see there needs to be a better system in place. All they said to me was to be sure nobody gets in without a ticket.

"Whether I like it or not, I have to take on extra jobs right now," he continued. "Last month my wife was killed by a drunken driver. I'm a single parent now and it's really a tough time for me and my boy. During the day I'm an appraiser and at night I'm a security guard for the Mighty Ducks, so I hardly have any time to be with my son. Your story from *Chicken Soup for the Soul* moved me so deeply and is a reminder that I need to let my son know that I love him and how much he means to me.

"By the way," he said enthusiastically, "I got one of these Blue Ribbons at a fancy event about eight years ago. It really made a difference to me. I still have that ribbon on my mirror. I look at it every day and it reminds me that I am somebody. Would you mind autographing my copy of *Chicken Soup for the Soul?*"

My heart melted as I listened to this giant man reveal his deepest feelings. "I'd be honored to autograph your book," I said tenderly. I looked up at his kind face and wrote in the book, "Dear Larry, You're a kind and loving father. Thank you for the difference you make."

Tears filled his eyes when I showed him what I had written. We gave each other a warm and lasting hug, as if we had known one another for a lifetime. As I walked away, I made eye contact with Denise. She was headed directly toward Larry with a Blue Ribbon in her hand.

Denise was once again her usual loving self. I watched her speak to Larry and place a second Blue Ribbon above the one he had just received. His face beamed.

Later, Denise and I strolled out of the convention hall, arm in arm. "I can't believe what just happened," she reflected. "I was so wrong about this man. I told him how hurt and angry I had felt when he was so abrupt with me. Almost in the same breath, I told him how much I now appreciated the difficult job he had. That's when he shared with me that his wife had just been killed. I was shocked and moved to tears. All I could think to do was to ask him for a hug. When we embraced, he expressed how sorry he was for having been so rude to me.

"When you told me earlier that I would acknowledge Mr. Gestapo with a Blue Ribbon before the day was out, I couldn't even imagine that happening. I think I'm beginning to understand," Denise said introspectively. "From now on, I will think twice before making snap decisions about anyone. Instead, I will always remember that everyone makes a difference."

Denise Wright — 1996

7

Acknowledging Frances

Dear Helice,

Please allow me to say the things I could not say to you last night at your Difference Makers musical presentation.

I have seen my wife, Frances, work on your project for over ten years. She would bring home the Blue Ribbons and get our two children to help her cut and package them so that you could meet your deadlines (she never had enough time to do them during her normal working hours at HGH).

As our children worked on the ribbons, she would tell them about "Helice, The First Lady of Acknowledgement." As you mentioned during the musical, cutting the Blue Ribbons MUST be a labor of love. And this is the message Frances has always delivered to our kids.

Who I Am Makes A Difference

Thoughout the years, I too heard about you, but could not truly appreciate who you were until last night (I have, by the way, seen Zig Ziglar several times, listened to Dennis Waitley and read Stephen Covey for years). As I listened to you, I realized that you have an uncanny ability to evoke the feelings that we all tend to hold in. I had tears running down my cheeks the entire evening. When I tried to tell Frances why she makes such a difference to me, I could barely speak. It was then that I realized that these emotions are truly from the heart!

Throughout my life I have said, all I want to do is make a difference. You are living the dream and are a model for me to know that I can too.

In closing, I would like to say thank you for the opportunity to hear your musical and to meet you. You have made a difference to someone I love very much and to the 'kids' she works with at HGH.

Today I am searching for someone to give my remaining ribbon to. Thank you for the difference you make to me.

James E. Stone
2 July, 1996

HGH, The Home for the Guiding Hands,
under the expert guidance of Frances Stone,
has been cutting and packaging our Blue Ribbons since 1986.

8

From Shower to Stage

Life is either a daring adventure or nothing at all.
— Helen Keller

For years one of my goals has been to take opera lessons. I really wanted to sing, but I was scared. Singing in the shower had become my vocal sanctuary.

Very early one Sunday morning, the doorbell rang. I jumped up and grabbed my bathrobe. Wiping the sleep from my eyes, I peeked out the window and saw my friend Helice. Still sleepy, I yawned as I was opening the door.

"Hi," Helice beamed. "May I come in?"

"Sure," I said, opening the door wider.

"I heard that you sing songs from Phantom of the Opera. Is that right?"

"Well...yes," I hesitated. "I know the song *All I Ask of You.*"

"Good. Sing a line of the song for me. I love that song...I have to hear it."

"Right now? I just woke up and my voice isn't even warmed up."

"Yes, right now!" insisted Helice. "I don't care what your voice sounds like. Just sing me one line!"

Well, I knew the song, but never felt very comfortable singing in front of people. I wasn't expecting to do a command performance at this hour of the morning. However, what I also knew was that Helice Bridges represents only unconditional love and support. Knowing that, I began to sing.

I had sung only one line when Helice announced, "Terrific! I'm writing a musical and you're in it. I love that song. I'll figure out a way to write the song into the script. Besides, I need help in designing this musical and you know music. Will you help me?"

It was all too fast for me to say no. Helice gave me no time to tell her that I only sang in the shower and didn't know much about music. She swept me up in her enthusiasm. Minutes later we were sitting on the floor co-creating her entire show.

I was surprised at how excited I was. I had never realized how much I had wanted to sing until that very moment. It only took me a few seconds to know who the perfect partner would be for this duet. It had to be Doug Morgan. He is not only a great musician and singer, but a friend I could count on to help me. I knew that I would feel safe if he were singing beside me. I was thrilled when he said YES!

Then Helice told me that the show would be in three weeks. Doug and I had to get started right away.

That's Helice's style...she has an idea, decides to do it, and *voila,* before you know it, you're doing something you never thought possible. Besides, there was nothing to lose and everything to gain. No matter how I sounded, Helice would say, "Thank you! You're very courageous and you were terrific!"

The night of the musical I was petrified. Yet, it became such an incredible experience when I received so much support from everyone in the cast. My singing was beautiful, except that I hummed two entire lines because I completely forgot the words! Nonetheless, I kept my composure and felt proud of my accomplishment. Doug's brilliant coaching, magnificent voice and friendship, along with the love and support of the audience, encouraged me to *finally* take singing lessons.

Helice called to announce that, because of the remarkable success of the first show, she had been invited to do the show at a major theater in downtown San Diego. Driving down to look at the theater, my fears returned. "Helice, now that your show will be held in a big theater, I'll understand if you want to get a professional to take my place."

"You... not in my show? Of course, you'll be in the show! That's what this whole thing is about...making dreams come true!" Helice insisted. And, that was that!

A month later, I was on the big stage. The only rehearsal was just hours before the performance. When

I sang my song for the cast, I was overwhelmed by the applause. I knew I was in my element.

The curtain went up and there I was with the spotlight on me. I couldn't see the audience, but I knew the house was packed. Just as I was about to sing, Helice stepped over to me and lovingly said, "Tell us your dream."

"I have always been afraid of singing in public. I was sure I would make mistakes and people would laugh at me. Then, I even thought, if I were really good, people would be envious. Until two months ago, I had only sung in the shower. Then, out of the blue, Helice invited me to sing in her musical. Tonight is only the second time that I've ever performed in front of an audience. Now, I'm taking singing lessons and my coach has invited me to be in a professional opera company."

When I began to sing, I was absolutely elated. I felt safe, supported and loved. All that was inside of me came forth in a burst of song that lifted me to the height of my spirit. For those few moments, I transcended time and space. When I hit the last note, the audience jumped to their feet and exploded with applause. I received a standing ovation!

Later, Helice told me that, by my example, I had brought everyone in the audience to the height of their greatness. It was so exciting for me to know that I just went for it — from shower to stage. There were other great singers that night, all of whom had received a standing ovation sometime during their career. *But, tonight, the standing ovation was mine.* Helice's belief in my dream had inspired something more powerful than the notes and the music — she had brought out the sound of God...the true joy within me.

Elizabeth Grow

9

Watch Out For Miracles —
They're Everywhere

Each day comes bearing its gifts. Untie the ribbons.
— Ann Ruth Schabadar

The security guard smiled a radiant hello as he opened the door for me. I smiled back, and said, "Thank you," and hurried into my bank. I had so much on my mind. My office floor was stacked with papers and files that desperately needed organizing. There were bills to be paid, phone calls to be returned and preparations to be completed for a meeting the following day. The book I wanted to write would, once again, have to be put on hold until I found a way to handle these never ending details which totally consumed my life.

Handing my deposit to the teller, I began to think about the security guard at the front door. Security guards often come and go at our bank. Each had his own personality, but none had a smile like this one or had ever opened the door for me. His brilliance nearly took my breath away. I wanted to stop and give him a Blue Ribbon, but clearly felt that I had no time.

Anxious to get back to the work at hand, I raced out of the bank, smiled, and waved a quick thank you to the security guard. I felt the sunshine of the day bathing my face and the salt air from the Pacific Ocean fill my nostrils. The sky was clear, the day was magical and I knew I could easily linger here for hours. I heard a clear voice inside my head say, "No time to stop and smell the roses."

Just as I was about to unlock my car door, I felt a mysterious heat against my back, gently coaxing me to turn around. Never before had I felt such warmth, which seemed to magnetically turn me in the direction that I needed to face.

In front of me was the security guard, sitting on his stool and smiling back at me. Before I realized it, I was walking toward him. "Hi, my name is Helice. What's yours?"

"Ed," he said confidently.

"Well, I'm proud to meet you Ed," I said, reaching to shake his hand. "How long have you had this job?"

"Two weeks."

"Do you like it?"

"No, not really. It's boring sitting here. But, at least it's outside in a beautiful area. I could have been working inside the convention center today, so I guess this is a lot better. Besides, I've made up a game that is fun and keeps me smiling. When there are only a few cars pulling into the lot, I run over to the front of the bank, smile at the customers, and open the door for them."

"It really felt great when you did that for me. In fact, I kept thinking about your smile and courtesy while I was waiting in line to make my deposit. What do you do when you're not working this job?" I asked, always curious about who people are inside their uniforms.

His eyes lit up as soon as I inquired. "I'm a medical assistant at a local hospital. I do sonograms and prep patients for the doctors."

"I can tell by looking at your face that that's your real passion, isn't it?"

Ed sat up tall, and his entire body lit up like a Christmas tree. "What I do at the hospital brings me the most joy. I wish they would schedule more hours for me."

"You're truly a great asset to anyone you work for," I said as I reached into my purse and pulled out three Blue Ribbons. "Ed, I appreciate your creativity, your desire to make a difference and the fact that, as often as you can, you are living your passion."

I placed the Blue Ribbon above his heart, pointing upwards toward all his dreams coming true. "Continue to go for your dreams, Ed, the ones that feed your soul. Always remember that I will have my hand on your shoulder cheering you on and reminding you that *Who You Are Makes a Difference.* And would you cheer me on too? You see, it is my deepest wish that all 265 million Americans will be acknowledged with a Blue Ribbon before the year 2000!"

"Wow, go for it!" he exclaimed. "I can get behind that dream!"

"Thanks," I gleamed. "Hope to see you again soon."

I had only taken a few steps toward my car when I heard Ed shout, "Oh, by the way, there are miracles occurring everywhere. Watch for the miracles!"

Curious, I turned toward him once again, "Have you experienced a miracle?"

"Sure have," he said.

"Tell me about it."

"About three years ago a car ran into me while I was walking down the street. It knocked me through a brick wall. All the doctors told me that both my legs had to be amputated. I refused to believe them! Since then, I've had a number of operations. Now I'm walking again and only have a corrective shoe on this one foot," Ed said as he pulled up his pant leg, revealing a shoe with a metal brace.

"What made you believe you could walk again?"

"I've never been one to give up. Just tell me I can't do something and I'll prove to you that I can! I might get bored doing this bank job, but I can't complain about my life. I'm alive, I'm walking and I'm watching my child grow up. I'm going to give these extra Blue Ribbons to my wife and son.

"Oh, I missed greeting those two people who just walked past us," Ed said as he turned away from me and quickly headed in the direction of the door.

"I'll never forget you, Ed," I shouted.

I walked slowly back to my car. I unlocked the door, slid into the driver's seat, but didn't start the car. Suddenly I had no desire to get back to the details waiting for me. Instead, I began to think about what Ed had just taught me.

Despite his physical condition, Ed had decided that he would walk on his own two feet. He didn't let the circumstances, the doctors, or anyone tell him he couldn't do it. I too, have an enormous ability to focus and achieve my dreams... no matter what people tell me. However, I wondered if I could muster up Ed's type of courage in the face of so much physical pain and uncertainty.

My thoughts drifted to a conversation that I had only the night before. My friend told me of a problem he had been dealing with on both a physical and an emotional level. I wish that he could have Ed's conviction. Suddenly I realized I was thinking about my friend's situation rather than focusing on mine. In that moment, I understood that it was I who needed Ed's unwavering conviction.

I felt as though I had just been hit over the head with a two by four. How could I allow myself to be consumed with the thoughts that I had no time to write my book or to live my own life passionately? Wasn't I the one who encouraged everyone else to live their passion? Who was I to tell others to pursue their dreams when I was not fully living mine?

As proud as I was of my ability to move forward in the face of uncertainty, it was clear that I had not quieted the chatter that consumed my mind. Ed, I know you wanted me to learn today that my brick walls are only illusions. That my inner thoughts could either amputate my spirit or inspire me to walk my talk. I know my thoughts are always my choice and not a result of outside circumstances. That just like you, I can achieve anything that I want and that you will always be on my shoulder cheering me on.

My inner dialogue loudly proclaimed, "Look what you've done. You've wasted all this time when you should be home, writing your book. But you can't get started until you clean up the mess on your desk, and the files need organizing..."

"Buzz off! There's nothing I have to do right now except to realize that I am in charge!"

The chatter stopped immediately. I was left with a sense of peace, certainty and knowing. No longer would the clutter of details stand in the way of living my vision, writing my book and making my contribution to the world.

I glanced across the parking lot and saw Ed opening the door for another customer. I knew that Ed was doing much more than that. He was an angel, who only moments before, had opened the vault to the treasures lying deep in my soul.

Perhaps Ed had a special gift for every customer with whom he came in contact. After all, it was Ed who shouted to me — "Watch out for miracles. Miracles are everywhere!"

Helice — 1996

10

Dare to Dream!

I will not live a half-hearted life
doubting my deepest desires,
hesitant to follow my dreams,
or afraid to discover my greatness.

I may have an endless stream of questions;
Am I worthy? Will I fail?
Do I have what it takes?
Will I be left alone with nothing?

*The truth is, this can only happen if I don't
follow my dreams.
For what is more distressing than a dream that
might have been?
What causes more regret than the sorrow of
never having risked?
And what could be lonelier than living the life
of somebody else?*

*I was born to move boldly towards my highest dreams,
bringing my most cherished desires to life.
There is a voice inside of me that proclaims;
I am here to remember who I really am!
I am here to love and be loved! I am here to be fully alive!
I am here to make a difference in this world!*

*I will wait no longer.
I know that my deepest desires arise from a source
within me that knows how to fulfill them.
Remembering this, I leap courageously
into the unknown with faith,
bringing my dreams to life, and inspiring others
to do the same.*

Diana Loomans

11

A Little Time and a Few Kind Words

You will find as you look back upon your life, that the moments that stand out, the moments you have really lived, are the moments when you have done things in the spirit of love.

— Henry Drummond

Dear Dad,

The most precious saying from you was always given in response to my question, "Dad, what do you want for Christmas or your birthday?" Your response was always the same..."Just a little time and a few kind words."

As a teenager, this response used to really infuriate me because I didn't want to have anything to do with you. You see, when you were an alcoholic, I had a tremendous resentment towards you for never being the father I had always dreamed of. I *would rather have bought you a tie or something that was "quick and easy" as opposed to spending any time with you. As much as I hated you for your drinking while I was growing up, I too became an alcoholic.*

Today Dad, I often think of the most memorable gift you ever gave me. It involved just a little time and not even a word. It was at Christmas, the last one we spent together before you died. I am so grateful today for the awareness that God graced us with that day.

It was Christmas morning, 1983. Our family gathered together in the living room just as we had on many other Christmas mornings...but something about this one was different. For one thing, both you and I were sober! I watched Glenn begin his usual tradition of gathering the gifts and anxiously giving them out to me, Karen, you and Mom.

You sat back in your chair observing the rest of us seated together on the couch across from you. You were so calm and serene and didn't have any attachment to opening your presents. Instead, you watched closely and observed how your family was celebrating Christmas.

As I watched you, Dad, I noticed a special twinkle in your eye. You were content to soak up the moment and grateful to be with us. It was clear to me that your real gift was simply being with your family.

When all the presents were unwrapped, Glenn, Karen and Mom left the room. It was just you and me. Dad, you got up slowly from your chair and calmly sauntered over and sat on the couch next to me. We connected eye to eye, didn't say a word, and yet we both began to cry at the same moment.

Without words there was a knowing. You see, we had given each other the gift we both really wanted. For the first time in my life, I felt that I had a father who loved me and his family unconditionally. You also knew that you had a son and a family who truly loved you unconditionally.

Today, I understand the value of your saying," Just a little time and a few kind words." I would gladly give up everything I own materially today just to spend a little time and have a few kind words with you again. Growing up, I always wanted you to be proud of me, but now it is I who want you to know how proud I am of you. Your values of love, family, God and country are something that would make this world a much better place if we all put them to practice in our daily lives.

Dad, I thank you for teaching me the most precious lesson that life has to offer. We are all here for only a short while. May we never get caught up in acquiring things and forget the most precious gifts...our families and each other.

Thank you for the many magical moments and gifts that words could never express. I love you Dad...forever!

Michael — 1996

written by: Michael Price

12

My Dad

When I was young
I asked my dad
About my life
And who I am

He smiled and sighed
And kind of laughed
And sat me on his
Warm soft lap

When I was young
I asked my dad
To come explore
So he found me an ocean
Of shell and coral

I asked my dad
What would we do
With the shell picked
From the sea

In the palm of his hand
He cradled my prize
And looked me straight
In my excited eyes

"My daughter", he said
"Inside of that shell,
I'll paint you a world
Full of dreams

And I'll coat it with love
Excitement and joy
And many other good things."

And now as I sit
And I look at my shell
It's plain for me to see

That all of my successes
And all of my joys
Came from the love
My dad had for me

Helice Bridges

13

Focus On What's Working

To help people reach their highest potential, catch them doing something right.
— Ken Blanchard and Spencer Johnson, M.D.
Co-authors, *The One Minute Manager*

Linda Theis is an exceptional school teacher. She continuously looks for ways to bring out the greatness in all her students. In 1983, she invited me to speak to her class of 8th grade students. Only a week earlier, I had the privilege of watching her students acknowledge one another with the Blue Ribbons. This day I would no longer be an observer, instead I would be communicating the importance of acknowledgement to thirty teenagers.

This was my *first* speech ever. I had so many knots in my neck, from fear that I would not do a good job, that I had to get a massage before and after this half hour program. I entered the classroom shaking and stood in the front of the room. The students smiled up at me. Each was wearing a Blue Ribbon. I began to relax. My attention went directly to Danny.

"Danny, I see you're wearing a Blue Ribbon. Didn't you tell me last week that you flunked your math test, your father took away your allowance, and your girl-friend broke up with you? How is it that you are able to wear this Blue Ribbon that says *Who I Am Makes a Difference?*"

"That's right," Danny replied. "But last week you told us all to acknowledge ourselves for what we did *right* and to give ourselves a pat on the back. So I gave myself a pat on the back for getting up on time for school, remembering to take my books to school, feeding my dog and for saying hello to an old friend. I felt so good, I even decided to open my math book and study. I got an "A" in math. I have two girlfriends now and my father was so impressed, he doubled my allowance."

Helice Bridges

14

Are You an Angel?

Whatever we have accomplished has been because other people have helped us.

— Walt Disney

My keys jingled in my hand as I walked across the parking lot on my way to the car. My business meeting had been very successful and I had the feeling that this particular day was going to continue on a great note.

"Excuse me. 'Scuse me," I heard someone shout. I looked around and saw a very shabbily dressed woman standing by an old car next to mine.

"Yes?" I responded with a smile.

"My car won't start." She said. "I wonder if you could give me a ride home? It's only a few blocks away." I had a little time before my next appointment, so I invited her to get in. As she walked toward the passenger side of my car, I noticed that she was limping badly. As soon as she got in, I could sense that she needed someone to talk to. "What's your name?" I asked. "My name is Andrea," she began. In the short time that it took to drive those few blocks, I became engrossed in a story which I could hardly believe.

We remained in my car long after we arrived at her house. She told me of her boyfriend whom she had just thrown out the day before. Reluctantly, she admitted that he was the one who had broken her leg six months ago. I was astounded that she was still limping so badly, even after that amount of time. She said she had loved him so much, that until now she had been willing to tolerate his constant abuse. Finally, yesterday, Andrea had come to understand why her 15 year old daughter had refused to come home from Texas as long as he was living at their home.

"I hadn't been getting along with my daughter," she cried. "She is so angry with me for tolerating his put downs and beatings. I'm such a failure at everything in life."

"Andrea, why don't you call her and tell her that you miss her and how much she really means to you? Although you feel you haven't been such a great mom, let her know that you've always done the best you knew how." Andrea nodded in agreement.

"I'm a parent too, and my children and I are continuously learning how to communicate with more love and compassion. I've taken a lot of personal growth trainings which have greatly helped me to relax, listen more, and acknowledge others and their feelings. I've learned to say what's on my mind without blowing up. I really know how challenging life can be."

"I don't know what it is, but I feel really comfortable with you," Andrea said.

I smiled as I reached into my purse and pulled out some Blue Ribbons. "Andrea, I have this Blue Ribbon for you that says *Who I Am Makes a Difference.* You have really made a difference in my life today. Thank you for being so open and willing to lean on someone for support."

Andrea began to cry. "Are you an angel?" she asked. "Did God send you to me to tell me these wonderful things?"

I was taken aback by her question. I looked directly in her eyes and said, "Well, Andrea, I guess so 'cause here I am."

In that moment, I reflected on the many people who had recently come into my life whom I considered as angels, too.

We hugged like old friends. I pulled out a tissue from my purse and gently wiped away her tears. She beamed with a new confidence. Her radiant face outshined her shabby clothes.

I watched her as she seemed to glide, limp and all, down the pathway to her house and into what I knew would be her new life.

Pat Farrell — 1996

15

Last Words of Love

Feeling unloved is the worst poverty in the world.
— Mother Teresa

As a professional speaker, I often bring Blue Ribbons to use at my talks even though I don't always get to use them. At one particular meeting, I demonstrated the Blue Ribbon Ceremony with the group, then invited each person in the group to acknowledge the person they were with.

Afterwards, a woman tearfully shared that her husband had looked right into her eyes and told her, for the first time in their 25 years of marriage, that she was beautiful, and that he was so glad she had chosen him as her husband. She went on to say that he even told her that she was a wonderful cook and had taken such good care of him and their home. Lastly, he told her how very much he had loved her all these years.

Everyone in the room listened on when she explained that her husband was a man of very few words. Harry is the type who, if asked, "Do you love me?" could only reply, "Would I be here if I didn't love you?"

It was truly a moving evening, once again reminding me of the power and magic of the Blue Ribbon.

A few months later, I stopped by to visit a friend whom I hadn't seen in a long time. We chatted for a bit in her shop and just as I was about to leave, another woman came through the door. My friend looked at me and said, "Oh, Rita, I'd like to introduce you to my friend Betty. She works for me part time. Betty, this is Rita Kahn, a long-time friend of mine."

Betty looked at me and turned *white.* "Oh, my God!" she exclaimed. "I don't believe it. I've been looking for you for months! I don't know if you remember me and my husband. We were first time guests at an organization where you spoke six months ago. You taught us the *Who I Am Makes a Difference* Blue Ribbon Ceremony. After my husband and I acknowledged each other, I shared in front of the group that my husband, who hardly ever communicated affectionately, told me how much he loved me and was so glad and grateful that I had chosen him as my husband."

"Well, of course," I smiled and shook my head yes. "Of course. How could I forget that evening or his sharing. He was so genuine and sweet when he stood next to you and thanked me for giving him the opportunity to declare his love for you in front of everyone. I speak to groups and organizations all over the country and don't always get to do the Blue Ribbon Ceremony.

For some reason that night, I was inspired to bring the ribbons along and use them. Your husband's sincerity left an impact on me that I haven't forgotten."

"Well," she said, "I've been wanting to find you to thank you for that evening and the Blue Ribbon experience. You see, my husband died of a heart attack the *very next day*. Now I keep that ribbon on my dresser where I can see it everyday. I guess I always knew he loved me, but hearing him say it in front of everyone that night was so very special. My God, if you had never done that Blue Ribbon Ceremony, I might have wondered the rest of my life if I had really made a difference to Harry. Now, every time I look at that ribbon, it reminds me of Harry's face, his smile and his last words of love.

Rita Kahn — 1985

16

My Momma

Dearest Mom,

You are radiant, loving, blissful, energetic, funny, playful and invigorating.

I remember the secret place you took me to eat lobster when I was only 6 years old. You taught me how to eat lobster right out of the shell. I watched you crack the claws, and with the smallest fork I'd ever seen, pull out a long thick thread of white delicious meat. Then you taught me how I could do the same.

I remember your hair pulled back, rolled up on the sides of your head and held together by hair pins. You always wore beautiful suits with padded shoulders that accentuated your small waistline. Ever since I was a small child, I felt everything was perfect when I was around you.

When I was 12 years old, you asked me to help you study so that you could pass your real estate test. We sat on the porch, drank lots of lemonade, and perspired under the hot

Florida sun. I asked you the test questions and you answered the best you could. It was so much fun doing that together.

You passed your test, went to work for someone and really did a great job. A year later, I helped you study for your broker's license. Once again you passed and opened your own real estate office. I can still remember reading the name on the building — ROTH REALTY — and thinking, "That's my mom!"

The office was big. You bought about 25 desks at the Goodwill — not one chair or desk matched. But it didn't make any difference to you. You always made magic out of everything you did.

People around you loved you. Why shouldn't they — you were a sparkle, a shining light. You pulled off deals that no one thought possible. You even found people on the street who had no jobs, took them in, taught them real estate and helped close their deals. Under your guidance, they made money and gained their self respect.

Whatever I needed, you helped me, too. It is because of you and Dad that I am who I am.

When I left my successful real estate practice at the age of 38, I called you with my Blue Ribbon idea? You said, "Sweetheart, you must get a <u>real job</u>. It's nice to tell people they matter and give them Blue Ribbons — but you're not making a living doing that. Go back to selling real estate or become a teacher."

"No, Mom. I can't do anything but this. This is my life and I cannot stop. I must tell people that they matter and give them a Blue Ribbon."

Every week you would call me with a new job idea and every week I would say, "No, — but thanks anyway."

I remember the day you called me up and said, "Honey, I've got the perfect job for you. I read about it in the newspaper. It's a multi-level pie company."

"A what?" I laughed. "Mom..." I started to say.

Before I could finish my sentence, you burst out laughing. Within a few seconds we literally were rolling on the floor laughing our hearts out. Through your laughter, you could hardly spit out the words..."O.K., I understand. You're not going to listen to me. You're going to keep putting these Blue Ribbons on people for the rest of your life. The pie company was my very last attempt. From now on I'll leave you alone."

And you kept your word. From that time on, you only encouraged me to continue to go for my dreams and reminded me..."Baby, you can do anything! I believe in you!"

Mom, you are now 85 years old and living in a nursing home. Sometimes when I visit you, I see a spark in your eyes and, for a fraction of a moment, I think you still remember who I am. Mostly you stare off in the distance, living in some remote place deep within that keeps your soul locked in jail. I can feel your caged hurt and disappointment at what your body has done to you.

Yet to me you are still as beautiful as ever. I can still hear you cheering me on and honoring my quest to acknowledge people. I can still feel your hand on my shoulder. I can still see your sparkling eyes.

And I remember the times when you felt that you were not good enough because you didn't have a college degree or make a million dollars. You felt that you needed a diploma to know that you were smart. Well Momma, some people were not meant to make a million dollars or get a college degree — they were meant to be great parents like you and Dad. To me, that's what wealth is really about.

Who I Am Makes A Difference

With your and Dad's love and support, I, too, have brought love to everything and everyone I've touched. No matter the thousands of mistakes I have made in these past 17 years, the frustrations or confusion I have felt — I have learned to keep on keeping on — just like you. I have even learned an important lesson along the way — to love and forgive myself.

You and Daddy always cheered me on for my dreams, hugged me and inspired me through your actions. You showed me how to be a responsible, stimulating, caring, fun, joyful, compassionate, loving and authentic person.

Everything that you gave me could not be earned through a diploma or a huge bank account. Momma, you gave me my life, my dream and my knowing that everything I will ever do always makes a difference.

Love,
Helice

17

Momma Nan's Warriors

When we began, 31 percent of all fifth graders indicated attitudes in favor of gangs and drugs. At the end of the program, only 7 percent indicated at risk attitudes.

—Ernie Paculba,
Coordinator, Gang Alternative Program,
Los Angeles Unified School District,
State Task Force on Gangs and Drugs, 1989

"We've been reading your *Who You Are Makes a Difference* story from *Chicken Soup for the Soul* at our various trainings," Keith said. "Brad, one of our trainers, passed your story on to some people from his home town of Fresno. Now he tells me everywhere he goes in his town, people are acknowledging one another with your Blue Ribbons. He told me a very powerful story that I thought would be important to pass on to you.

"Brad went to acknowledge his Pastor and his wife, affectionately known as Momma Nan. Momma Nan was very ill at the time Brad presented her with her first Blue Ribbon. The acknowledgement touched her so deeply that she requested, when her time came, that *everyone* at her funeral receive a Blue Ribbon. Shortly thereafter, Momma Nan passed on. As she was laid to rest, everyone turned to a person next to them and placed a Blue Ribbon just above their heart."

Keith continued, "We were all so moved by this very special acknowledgement, that we'd like you, as the originator, to be the key-note speaker at our awards banquet in a few months. I'll set up a luncheon meeting prior to the banquet, so that you can met Pastor T, who is anxious to tell you his story." I was moved by what I had heard and immediately agreed to fly to Fresno.

When I arrived, the first thing I saw was a man with a sign that said, "Welcome to Fresno, Helice Bridges. *Who You Are Makes a Difference!*" I was touched by the extraordinary acknowledgement. He walked over to me and introduced himself, "Hi, I'm Brad and I've been pinning your Blue Ribbons on people all over Fresno."

After a short ride, Brad and I entered an elegant restaurant, where I was greeted enthusiastically by Pastor T, Steve and Bubba. Pastor T had brought a large portrait of his wife, Nan, which was proudly displayed at our table. He began by saying, "I wanted everyone here to meet you today. There was quite a story behind how Momma Nan declared her wish for a Blue Ribbon Ceremony at her funeral. Brad, why don't you begin telling Helice what happened."

"It was at a training session in Stockton when I first heard your story and received my Blue Ribbon. The experience was so powerful that I decided to include the story and the ceremony in all our Fresno training sessions."

Steve piped in, "When I heard Brad tell your story, I immediately knew that I had to give a Blue Ribbon to my wife. You see, I've been working 16 to 18 hours a day. I get home very late and don't have much time to spend with her. She's diabetic and has been getting worse. By the time I get home, I'm wiped out and don't have the patience to give her the attention she deserves. That's all changed now.

"After Brad's training session, I came home, sat beside my wife and acknowledged her with the Blue Ribbon. I told her how very much I loved and cared about her. I said that I realized how difficult it must be for her when I'm not around to help. We spoke for a very long time and talked about how to cherish the time we do have together. I've even been coming home from work earlier for the past month. To tell you the truth, that Blue Ribbon Ceremony saved our marriage.

"But I didn't stop there. I decided it was time for me to also mend the relationship with my father. Actually, we hadn't spoken in over five years. I called him, and to my surprise, he accepted my invitation to have breakfast together. For days, I rehearsed what I would say to him and how I would present the Blue Ribbon. I imagined the good that could come out of it. Boy, was I ever nervous.

"As soon as we ordered breakfast, I took out a Blue Ribbon and just went for it. I thought it would be difficult, but was surprised at how words of appreciation sprang from my lips. He listened intently as I told him how sorry I was for giving him a hard time. The more I spoke, the more his eyes welled up with tears. My father *never* cried. Finally, I placed the Blue Ribbon above his heart. By then we were both sobbing. My father actually reached out and gave me a giant hug!

"Your *Who You Are Makes a Difference* story really hit a cord inside of me. The father in that story reminded me of myself. He only focused on what his son was doing wrong. I realized that I was doing the same thing to both my wife and Dad. When I read the story, it really opened up my eyes. Now everyday, life is different at work and at home. I now acknowledge people openly and sincerely. I'm always so amazed at what a difference it makes. I'm truly a changed person!

"I was on such a great roll, that I couldn't wait to acknowledge my friend Bubba." I focused my attention across the table on this huge, 350 pound man with a kind and gentle face. "I decided to acknowledge my friend Bubba," Steve continued, "and give him a Blue Ribbon."

Bubba immediately jumped in. "That's when everything started to change for me," Bubba spoke up. "First of all, I used to rattle when I walked because of all the guns I carried on me. Just a few years back, I flew drugs into Florida from South America. Since I've moved here, Pastor T has been determined to show me another way. For the past two years, he's been praying me into his church. I couldn't figure out why he wanted to put so much attention on a loser like me.

Believe it or not, I've been more afraid of Pastor T's love than of getting shot!"

"Pastor T had his own arsenal of warriors and my friend, Steve, was part of his tribe. The day Steve acknowledged me and told me how much I made a difference, I couldn't believe my ears. I couldn't believe that I had ever made a difference to anybody, ever in my life. I was only into surviving. But Steve and Pastor T were so sincere, I felt I *really* did make a difference.

"Knowing what an impact that little Blue Ribbon had on me, I thought that, just maybe, it could help the guys that were in the gangs. They did what they did just to feel important. These kids kill one another every day over nothing more than a Twinkie. They absolutely don't feel that they make any difference at all.

"I decided to gather up these throw-away kids and direct them into Pastor T's church. There ain't none of them tough enough to mess with me. When they came, I read your story to them. Then I passed out Blue Ribbons to every kid and gave them a chance to acknowledge one another. There wasn't a dry eye in the house. In fact, a week later, these kids, from different gangs, actually sat down and had dinner together. You can't imagine how miraculous a sight that was.

"These are hard nosed kids who don't appear to have any feelings. And yet, today, only two months after we first met at the church, 37 of the 42 kids that were at that church meeting are either back in school or have full time jobs."

Pastor T added, "These are the same kids who started to visit Momma Nan during her last days. They all insisted that they wanted to come to her bedside and pray for her because she had always made such a difference in their lives. There wasn't much room in our bedroom, but it didn't matter to those kids. Each day they would pile in, get down on their knees and pray. They did that right up until the day she passed on. It was because of what these kids did that Momma Nan requested your Blue Ribbons at her funeral.

"I have always known that the miracle of love could touch anyone or anything." Pastor T continued. "We now have living proof. The simple act of unconditional love reaches deep into the soul, healing the unseen wounds of even the greatest warriors."

18

Pass on the Love

A winner knows how much he still has to learn even when he is considered an expert by others.

— Linus Pauling

Have you ever slowed down to search for a street address and looked through your rear view mirror only to see an angry face giving you a stern look or shouting obscenities? It has happened to me from time to time over my forty years as a driver, but never have I had the opportunity to meet the person behind me face to face. Today was different.

As I was driving, the front bumper from the car behind me narrowly missed hitting me each time I slowed down. Thoughts ran through my mind like, "Oh God, please help me find a gas station soon! This poor gentleman behind me is becoming more frustrated by the minute, not to mention what a poor example I'm setting for my fellow drivers."

I wanted so much to stop my car, run over to him, and say, "Hi, my name is Helice Bridges. I'm actually a very nice lady. I wish that I could have remembered which street the gas station was on. I'm sorry for the frustration I've caused you."

After what seemed like an eternity, I finally spotted a gas station up ahead and turned in with a sigh of relief. To my surprise, the man was still right behind me. He pulled up to the pump next to mine. This was my golden opportunity.

I watched him walking toward the cashier and called out to him "Excuse me sir, I am hoping that you'll accept my apology for driving so slowly. I was trying to find the nearest gas station. I held a ribbon in my hands and said, "I have a Blue Ribbon that says *Who I Am Makes a Difference*. I'd like to give you this gift to thank you for your patience."

"Patience," the man snapped back, "you're honoring me for my patience? I'm a psychiatrist — you know, the professional who is supposed to keep his cool under any circumstances. Instead, here I am riding your back bumper and shouting obscenities under my breath. I have no patience. And now, out of nowhere, you come along and thank me for my patience," the man said looking frustrated and embarrassed.

"Well, you can *always* improve on anything," I smiled. "Isn't that what you remind your patients of each day?"

"Yes...I guess that's true. I've seen thousands of patients over the years improve their lives as a result of my help. I guess I'm no different, I can sure use your encouragement right now." He glanced down at the ribbon, looked me in the eye and said, "OK, I'll accept your gift."

Sam Mitchell smiled from ear to ear as I placed a Blue Ribbon over his heart right there in the middle of the busy gas station. I told him how much I appreciated having the chance to talk with him and encourage him to make all his best dreams come true.

He looked at the extra ribbons I handed him and read the Blue Ribbon instruction card with great interest. "It says that I am now a *Difference Maker*," he said with pride. "I will never forget you Helice Bridges," he said with a sincere look of gratitude as he gave me an unexpected embrace. "It's funny, I came here to fill up my tank and now I'm filled up in more ways than one! From now on, you can count on me to slow down, have more patience and pass on the love!"

I drove away with the continuing sense of renewal that comes from reaching out to a fellow human being, along with a whole new perspective on angry, rear-view drivers!

Helice — 1997

19

The Truck Driver

Let no one ever come to you without leaving better and happier.

— Mother Teresa

He was doing what he does every day. No big deal...or so he thought. Day in and day out, it's his job to lift heavy boxes off the truck and deliver them.

"Very impressive!" I thought, as I watched the truck driver pause, straighten his back and take in a deep breath before lifting each of the huge cartons.

I entered the high rise building in downtown San Diego and headed for the elevator. Following right behind me was the truck driver. I entered the elevator and stepped aside to make room for him and his cumbersome cargo.

"Hi," I smiled, pulling out a Blue Ribbon and turning to him. "I have a Blue Ribbon that says *Who I Am*

Makes a Difference and I would like to honor you for the brilliant way you bend and breathe. Would you accept my gift?"

The truck driver stood speechless and simply shrugged his weary shoulders.

"May I have permission to place it on you?" I asked.

"Slap it right there, baby!" the truck driver shouted as he pointed to his chest.

I placed the Blue Ribbon just above his heart, pointing upward toward all his dreams coming true.

"Y'know, lady, there oughta be more people in this world like you."

Hearing that, I quickly pulled out a few extra Blue Ribbons, handed them to him and said, "Here, go be one of them."

Since that eventful day in 1980, that truck driver's wish has been granted — for it has become the tradition to automatically pass on at least two extra Blue Ribbons with every acknowledgement.

Without his knowing it, the truck driver has made it possible for millions of additional people to be acknowledged. It has always been my dream that someday, somewhere, that truck driver will read this story and know that he inspired that tradition.

If you are reading this, Mr. Truck Driver, thank you from the bottom of my heart and know that I *was* listening.

Helice — 1982

20

I Am Somebody

No one can make you feel inferior without your permission.
— Eleanor Roosevelt

It was only a week following the 1992 Los Angeles riots, when I received a phone call to go to L.A. and teach *The Power of Acknowledgement* to members of two rival gangs.

"Sure," I responded quickly, "I'll come up right away."

Within a few days, I joined a team of prominent comedians, artists and photographers who had agreed to spend the week giving these young members of the Bloods and Crips their best tools for succeeding in life.

That night, the reality of what I was about to do the next day set in. What in the world was I doing in a place like this? I'd never worked with gang members or even seen a ghetto. I tossed and turned the entire night. Even worse, I had been selected to be the *first* trainer!

The following morning, I hid out in the corner of the room as sixty reluctant gang members, each wearing a leather jacket, were escorted into the room. Some slid down into their seats, others rolled their eyes backwards, or yawned. Most looked distant and unapproachable. One girl had pink rollers in her hair. She walked to a seat in the third row with her head down, arms crossed at her chest, mumbling under her breath. Within minutes after she sat down, she was sound asleep.

"What in the world am I going to do?" I thought. "Be authentic. Go with your gut! Believe that who you are *can* make a difference."

My eyes scanned the audience. Tough crowd was an understatement.

Suddenly I heard myself ask, "Have you ever seen someone walk into a room and everything about him says that he's important? There's something in the way he looks, stands and walks that declares to those around him that he matters. How would *you* like to be that person?"

No one spoke, moved or showed any sign that what I was saying was understood. I took in a silent breath and pointed to a young man in the last row. "Excuse me, would you be willing to come up here with me? May I have permission to coach you up to your greatness? It is my intention that you will always know you are somebody. Great champions like Kareem Abdul Jabaar have coaches. May I be that coach for you?"

He shrugged his shoulders, didn't say a word and strolled up to the front of the room. "Great! Thanks! Good! Now we can get started!" I declared.

"Get started with what?" I asked myself. I could feel the entire audience slicing me with their eyes, internally shouting, "Get on with it lady!"

Everything faded into the background except the six-foot-tall young man standing in front of me. "May I have permission to place my hands on your face, hands and knee?"

He shrugged his shoulders, and I took that to mean 'yes'. I placed my hands on both sides of his face, straightening his head so that it sat directly over his neck. Next I placed both of my hands on his wrists and lifted his hands out of his pockets, placing them gently at his side. Finally, I tapped his right knee with my fingers, giving him the opportunity to stand tall and proud. I looked directly at this brave young man, witnessing his magnificence, inner beauty and courage. "Thank you," I said sincerely. "I'm truly proud of you."

For only a moment, I turned my attention away from him and addressed the audience. No sooner than I began to speak, I noticed from the corner of my eye that he had quickly reverted back to his original position...head tilted back, hands in his pockets, right knee bent.

Without missing a beat, I walked toward him, gazed into his deep brown eyes, began adjusting his head, hands and leg, continuously saying, "Thank you! Good job! I appreciate your working with me!"

Each time I turned to face the audience, he went back to his original position. With acknowledging words, I continued to coach him to stand for his greatness. We repeated this process approximately twenty-five times. There was a magical flow between this young man and I — we were beyond time and space. I was honored that he continued to let me touch him, coach him and acknowledge him for nearly half an hour.

During the entire time, he stood his ground, yet was respectful of my coaching. I never saw him as a challenge. He was a privilege to be with and I admired his quiet toughness.

In the end, I presented him with a Blue Ribbon as a constant reminder that I really appreciated who he was. During this entire time, there was rapt attention from the audience.

I have no memory of the next two hours of my training. To this day, I only remember that the morning ended with my invitation to everyone to pair up and acknowledge one another with a Blue Ribbon. It never occurred to me, during their Blue Ribbon Ceremony, that I had invited a room full of sworn enemies to acknowledge one another.

They slapped Blue Ribbons on each other without much fanfare. I watched and wondered whether what I had done that day had made a difference. I drew a deep breath, looked into their eyes and I quietly prayed.

Four days passed before I would train them again. During that time, I observed them working with other great coaches. Every once in a while I would see some of them smile, shake a hand, or even take pride in what they were doing.

At the end of the week, they returned to me for the finale. As they entered the room, they looked even more withdrawn than the first day we met. The girl still had her pink rollers in her hair and found the same seat in the third row. As soon as she sat down, she dropped her head and closed her eyes. I wondered, had all of the contributions made by so many people during that week fallen on deaf ears?

Playing off an idea that I saw the comedians do that week to create stage presence, I announced to the room, "Before me is an imaginary line. In a moment, any one of you can come forward and stand in front of this line. When you do, stand proud, as I taught you the other day. I'll run to the back of the room. Watch the way I stand and model me. When you come to the line, stand behind it, head upright, hold your body tall, place your hands to your sides. Begin by saying 'Hi, my name is_____! Then I'd like everyone in the audience to simultaneously respond by saying 'Hi_____, YES!'"

"Okay, who wants to be first?"

I was shocked to see the girl with the pink rollers slowly lift her head and raise her hand. I smiled and motioned her to come to the front of the room. I watched her proudly stand behind the imaginary line. Quickly, I ran to the back of the room, standing in full view behind the audience, and invited her to imitate me. She did!

"Good morning. My name is Gloria," she said proudly.

"Good morning Gloria, YES!" everyone simultaneously shouted.

"Oh my God," I was thinking, "this *is* working!"

"Thank you Gloria. Now while you're up there, tell everyone what you are most proud of this week."

"Well, after you spoke to us the other day, I decided to tell my teacher that she no longer had permission to put me down when she spoke to me. I told her that I deserve respect as a student just as much as she deserves respect as a teacher. I told her that I didn't think that respect ought to go only one way and that maybe we could work together to do something about it."

My eyes were drawn to one of the teachers in the back of the room. Her neck had tightened and her face was flushed. I concluded that this was the teacher Gloria was speaking about.

"Acknowledge her with a Blue Ribbon," a young man in the back of the room whispered.

"What?" I strained to hear what he was saying.

"Acknowledge her and give her a Blue Ribbon," he said loudly.

Shocked, I took a Blue Ribbon from my pocket, acknowledged Gloria for her courage to ask for what she wanted and placed a Blue Ribbon over her heart. Everyone hooted, hollered, and applauded as Gloria and I hugged. She immediately took an empty seat in the front row. She was shining and sitting as proud as a peacock.

My eyes caught her teacher leaning against the back wall. "Would you care to be next?" I asked. "You bet I would!" she exclaimed as she marched to the front of the room.

"Please stand behind this imaginary line," I instructed. "I'll go to the back of the room. Thank you in advance for standing proud."

I ran to the back of the room. The teacher straightened her posture and blurted out, "Good morning, my name is Mrs. Wilson."

Once again, everyone shouted back in unison, "Good morning, Mrs. Wilson, YES!" *The room was electric.* It felt as though we were in the Super Bowl playoffs with everyone in the stadium cheering for both teams.

"Mrs. Wilson," I asked, "what are you most proud of?"

"I've been working at this school for over 23 years," she explained. "The girls lie, cheat and steal. No matter what, I still show up for them day in and day out." Then she paused, looked straight at Gloria, and said, "But girl, you're different and I've sure got a lot to learn from you!"

Mrs. Wilson reached out to Gloria and they hugged as the cheering in the room got even louder.

For the remaining two hours, every gang member came forward and acknowledged why they were proud of themselves. My tall friend was the last person to come forward. His head, hands and knee stayed in the old position — yet clearly his story spoke of the magnificence of who he had become in those four short days.

Who I Am Makes A Difference

"Until you acknowledged me the other day, I had only heard words that put me down. Every day of my life I've been told that I'm a nobody. I wanted so badly for my daddy to say I was someone special. I even worked hard and got A's and B's in school to show him I could be somebody. Nothin' I did made any difference. He would rather slap me on my butt than pat me on my back. When my dad left, I joined a gang. At least there... I am *somebody*."

"Then I realized something after you gave me that Blue Ribbon the other day. No matter what, you kept telling me that I mattered and you never gave up. What you said and did made a difference. I suddenly realized that I could stand on my own two feet and make a difference in my home and neighborhood.

"That afternoon I raced home and told my mom that I *never* wanted her to tell me that I'm lazy like my old man or tell herself that she's ugly. Then I told her to put out her cigarette, take the rollers out of her hair and get into something nice, because I was gonna take her out for a stroll."

"We walked down the street arm in arm — quiet like. I held my head up and I knew that people in the neighborhood were looking at us. *We were somebody.*"

Helice — 1992

21

Letter From Robert

Dear Helice,

You have created and have projected a multicolored, energized, uplifting force of possibility that mobilizes attention and change — an evolution of self and spirit.

As a result of this interchange, defenses evaporate. The recognition of self and others gathers momentum — the process has a life of its own.

Whether it is an audience, a group, or an individual, there is an acceptance and applause with the presence of who you are. Who you are creates a difference, an alteration of the experience of the present moment.

To the observer, the audience is transformed. Individually and collectively, there is change; disconnectedness becomes connectedness. There is a development of a common language. The relationship has a rhythm that changes the experience of time in the present. You are the artist, the sculptor of this.

Robert

Robert Dobrin, M.D., is an adult, adolescent and child psychiatrist practicing in Southern California

117

22

The Dance

There are people who put their dreams in a little box and say, "Yes, I've got dreams, of course. I've got dreams." Then they put the box away and bring it out once in a while to look in it, and yep, they're still there. These are great dreams, but they never even get out of the box. It takes an uncommon amount of guts to put your dreams on the line, to hold them up and say, "How good or bad am I?" That's where the courage comes in.

— Erma Bombeck

On a park bench — 200 feet above the roaring Pacific Ocean — I sat quietly, relaxing and breathing in the rays of the sun. The day was clear, calm, sweet. Sunset was only an hour away.

I noticed that on a bench only 50 feet further along the path was an older woman. She was frail and bent over from the weight of her shoulders. She had a large, witch-like beak nose. Despite her appearance, something about this woman drew me to her.

I walked to where she was seated, sat beside her, but I kept my focus on the ocean. For a very long time we sat in silence. Without thinking, I spontaneously turned to this old woman and quietly asked, "If we never saw each other again, what would you like me to know about who you really are?"

Tears rolled down her cheeks. "No one has ever cared that much about me," she sobbed. I placed my hand lightly on her shoulder to comfort her and said, "I care."

After introducing herself as Isabel, she whimpered, "Ever since I was a little girl, I have always wanted to be a ballerina. But my mother told me I was too clumsy and determined that it was a waste of money to give me dance lessons. "But I have a secret," she whispered, "I've never told anyone this before. You see, ever since I was four years old, I've been practicing my dance. I would hide in my closet and practice so my mother wouldn't see me."

"Isabel, show me your dance," I urged.

Isabel looked at me in surprise. "You want to see me dance?"

"Absolutely," I insisted.

That was when I saw the miracle. Isabel's face seemed to shed years of pain. Her face softened. She sat up proud, head erect, shoulders back. Then she stood up, turned and faced me. It was as if the world stood still for her. I could see it in her face. She wanted to dance and I was the audience that she had been waiting for all her life.

Isabel stood before me, took a long deep breath and relaxed. Only moments before, her brown eyes were sunk deep into her skull. Now they were bright and alive. Elegantly she pointed her toe forward while gracefully stretching out her hand. The move was masterful. She took my breath away. I was witnessing a miracle before my eyes. One minute, she was an ugly, old, miserable woman; the next, she was Cinderella wearing glass slippers.

Her dance took a lifetime to learn and only a moment to do. Isabel had fulfilled her life's dream. She had danced.

Isabel began to laugh and cry almost at the same time. In my presence, she had become the ballerina of her childhood dreams. We continued to speak about all the things that Isabel loved. I listened and hung on her every word. "You are a very great dancer, Isabel. I am proud to have met you." And I really meant it.

I never saw Isabel after that. I still remember smiling and waving good-bye to her. Since that day, I have taken the time to stop and acknowledge people every-where. I have asked them what their dreams are. I have cheered them on. Each time I do this, I witness a miracle. Like Isabel, people stand taller, smile and begin to believe in themselves and their dreams again. They begin to dance.

Helice — 1979

23

A Blue Ribbon Team

No man is an island, entire of itself; every man is a piece of the continent, a part of the main.
— John Donne, English Poet

Exhausted, depressed and discouraged, I left my dorm and headed straight for the cafeteria for a hot cup of coffee and a Hostess Ding Dong. In a few days, my finals would be behind me and I would forge into the world, a journalist at last. But at that very moment, the only thing that consumed me were fears of failing, disappointing my mom and never finding a job.

I put the coffee on my tray, changed my mind about the Ding Dong and opted for a cup of fresh fruit. I was fumbling for my money to pay the cashier when my eyes caught sight of a *Who I Am Makes a Difference* Blue Ribbon taped to the side of the cash register.

The cashier gave me my change as I inwardly repeated the phrase, *Who I Am Makes a Difference.* I carried my tray to a quiet table away from the other students. Sipping my coffee, I kept repeating the message. I was surprised when a wave of relaxation swept through my body releasing the pain in my neck and back. I leaned back, and closed my eyes dreaming...*I'm actually going to be a journalist soon!*

"I do make a difference! After all, I took a heavy load of classes and scored pretty well this last semester. Yes, I'm going to make it!" I continued to affirm.

Looking around the cafeteria, I observed the stressed out and depressed faces of the other students and made a note that only a few short minutes before I saw the Blue Ribbon, I felt and looked just like them. "Hmmm, interesting," I thought, "what a powerful statement."

I remember, several years later, proudly watching my little brother performing in his high school play. Little did I know that *The First Lady of Acknowledgement* was sitting beside me. I enthusiastically kept applauding long after everyone else had stopped. *The First Lady of Acknowledgement* noticed that I was smiling from ear to ear. "That's my little brother," I said with pride. "He's really something, isn't he?" The *Lady* smiled in agreement.

"Excuse me," I questioned. "I noticed that you're wearing a *Who I Am Makes a Difference* Blue Ribbon."

"Have you seen this ribbon before?" she asked.

"Actually, yes," I continued, "I first saw it taped to the cash register at San Diego State University. It was during final exams a few years ago. I was under incredible pressure to get good grades and a good job. When I read what it said, I thought about the statement for a moment. It hit me powerfully. Repeating the phrase in my mind seemed to suddenly wash away my fears and put a smile on my face. I couldn't quite explain it, but that's what happened. One minute I was discouraged, overloaded and drowning in fear and the next I was smiling, relaxed and focused on my future."

"Did you pass your tests?" she asked.

"Oh yes. I'm a free lance journalist now."

"Good for you!" the *Lady* applauded and pulled out three Blue Ribbons from her purse. My eyes got as wide as saucers looking at the ribbons.

"What's your name?" she inquired.

"Samantha," I answered.

"Samantha, I have a Blue Ribbon for you. Let this Blue Ribbon always remind you of the great difference you make with every word you write," the *Lady* said placing her hand on my shoulder. "I know your gift will impact people throughout the world. Remember, every time you look at this Blue Ribbon, and continually say the words, *Who I Am Makes a Difference,* it will give you the strength to make your dreams come true."

She placed the ribbon above my heart, handed me some extra ribbons and sat back as I told her about all the challenges I had overcome to educate myself and go for my dreams. I told her that I don't usually talk to strangers, but after seeing the Blue Ribbon, I knew I could talk with her.

My brother came running toward us. I stood up to meet him. "Good luck," the *Lady* said as she waved good-bye. "I hope we'll meet again someday."

From the corner of my eye, I noticed that she watched as I stood facing my little brother with a Blue Ribbon. "Tommy," I said, "I have this Blue Ribbon and I want you to know that you have the best personality and are the greatest dancer. You had so much fun on the stage tonight. Thanks for really going for it! Would you accept this gift?"

"Sure!" Tommy said standing taller.

"It goes above your heart toward all your dreams coming true."

"Wow, this is really neat. Where'd you get the ribbon?"

"From a lady I just met sitting next to me. Pretty terrific, huh?"

"Yeah, it's wonderful!" Tommy beamed.

I looked up and saw Mom entering the auditorium. Her nurse's uniform fell loosely on her slender frame. She worked nights since Dad left. Her loving smile always covered up the pain she felt inside. I knew how very much she hated missing Tommy's play.

Tommy and I gave Mom a big hug, rambling on about how great Tommy had done and how he hadn't even looked nervous on stage.

Tommy was a pretty sensitive young man and I knew that he wished things were easier for Mom. He took the Blue Ribbon I gave him off his shirt. "Mom," he said, "I have this Blue Ribbon for you. You always make a difference to me and I'm really glad you're here."

Tears flowed down our cheeks, as the three of us huddled tighter. "We've held it together during these hard times," Mom cried, "sometimes I forget how much you both mean to me, but there is no mistake about this moment. You are both so precious to me. Thank you for this lovely gift."

Tommy kissed Mom on the cheek just as a group of performers ran up to him yelling "Hey Tommy, we're all going out for ice cream."

"Yeah, coming in just a second."

"Hi, Mrs. Greer," Tommy's friends shouted, "where'd you get that Blue Ribbon — that's cool!" They ran off before she had a chance to answer.

Mom and I never had a lot of time to talk, but somehow this night was different. We spent hours laughing, crying and hugging as we shared our hopes, dreams and fears. Somehow, the Blue Ribbon experience gave us permission to express our deepest feelings.

My journalism jobs began taking me to cities far away from Mom and Tommy. Years passed — my career had been slow to get started. I had my good days and bad. The Blue Ribbon experience was tucked away deep in my heart and on occasion, I would look at it stuck to my mirror and repeat the words *Who I Am Makes a Difference*. Somehow it still calmed me down and helped me to believe.

I was a gifted writer. I knew that. But the world wasn't knocking my door down. The only thing good about the writing was the money I was making. What a price to pay!

After completing my most recent assignment in San Francisco, I hopped a plane back to San Diego. I looked forward to a relaxing flight, where I could sort things out and make some important decisions about my future. Just then, a robust man sat down next to me and changed my life. He was as big and jolly as Santa Claus. "Ho, Ho, Ho! My name is Bob Moss," he said. "Who are you?"

His strong, enthusiastic handshake jolted me out of my depression. "Samantha," I answered joyfully.

"Samantha, I'm glad to be seated next to you!"

As we buckled our seat belts, he asked me what I did. "I'm a free lance writer whose has had her ups and downs in the job market," I told him. "I wish I could get a good paying job with people who were making a difference. I just want to write inspiring stories. I know I'm a great writer, I just need a chance."

Bob listened as I rambled on. I discovered that Bob Moss was a professor at the University of California San Diego. He was on his way home after having completed a trip throughout the State of California speaking with under-privileged children from all backgrounds and nationalities. He told me that his message to young people is that they can be as successful as they choose. I watched as he reached inside his briefcase and pulled out a Blue Ribbon.

I gasped, "Where'd you get that ribbon?"

"From a lady in San Diego who acknowledges people wherever she goes. She donated 1500 ribbons to me so that I could honor the kids on my trip.

"This Blue Ribbon is just for you, Samantha. Whenever you look at it, always be reminded that you can do anything and that *Who You Are Makes a Difference!*"

My head began to whirl. This jolly Santa Claus' voice trailed off into the distance. I repeated in my head, "Samatha, you've got what it takes...keep going for your dreams.

Bob handed me two additional ribbons. I sat stunned for what seemed like a long time. Then I quietly turned to this jovial man seated next to me, gave him a hug and whispered in his ear, "I know exactly who these extra Blue Ribbons will go to."

Two nights later, I sat at my desk and wrote these letters to Mom and Tommy —

Dear Mom,

Enclosed is a "Who I Am Makes A Difference" Blue Ribbon just for you. Remember the time Tommy first gave you one? Mom, you deserve a million Blue Ribbons. You always believed in Tommy and me ever since we were little. You encouraged us to live our dreams — to become anything we wanted. You helped put us through college and never gave up, even when times were rough. I'm not going to ever give up either.

> *Your loving daughter, successfully brilliant and inspired journalist,*
> *Samantha.*

Dear Tommy,

I know that medical school is really difficult for you right now. Although I never told you, I was always afraid of flunking when I was in college. In fact, I was terrified most of the time, but I never told anyone. Yet, somehow I made it, but not without the help of you and Mom. You have always been my shining light. I have always admired your ability to go for what you believe in.

Enclosed is a "Who I Am Makes a Difference" Blue Ribbon. Remember the night I first gave you one? Remember when you passed it on to Mom? That was one of the happiest moments in my life. I felt that nothing could stop us. Believe it or not, that was seven years ago. I can't believe so much time has passed since you, Mom and I were together.

Tommy, although we live far apart, this Blue Ribbon is my way of saying that you are in my heart every day. I'm cheering you on to become the best doctor in the world. You, Mom and I, no matter our woes or our wins, we're a Blue Ribbon team.

Love,
Samantha — 1985

You Are A Child of God

Our deepest fear is not that we are inadequate.
Our deepest fear is that we are powerful beyond measure.
It is our light not our darkness that most frightens us.
We ask ourselves, who am I to be brilliant, gorgeous,
talented and fabulous?
Actually, who are you not to be?

You are a child of God.
Your playing small doesn't serve the world.
There's nothing enlightened about shrinking so that
other people won't feel insecure around you.
We were born to make manifest the glory of God
that is within us.

It's not just in some of us; it's in everyone.
And as we let our own light shine,
we unconsciously give other people
permission to do the same.

As we are liberated from our own fear;
our presence automatically liberates others.

Nelson Mandela
1994 Inaugural Address
Taken from *A Return to Love*
by: Marianne Williamson

24

Our Stand For Children

Nearing the completion of this book, I felt a hollow feeling inside of me...something was still missing. I couldn't put my finger on it. I leaned back in my chair, took in a deep breath and relaxed. Without realizing it, my hand reached back inside my desk drawer and pulled out a file. I casually opened it. Inside was the answer I had been looking for...the focus for publishing this book. Holding the contents in my hand, I became alive and passionate about making absolutely certain that *every* child throughout the world would live, dream and succeed in a world where they were safe, supported and loved. Most importantly, children would become an integral part of the decision making that would insure the success of this vision.

As I read *My Ten Rights as a Child,* I thought back to the first time I had held this paper in my hand. I had casually joined a meeting at the San Diego Chapter of the United Nations. About 10 people were seated around a table discussing the upcoming 1990 World Summit for Children to be held at the United Nations in New York City. Their goal was to have San Diego's children write letters to President Bush asking him to attend this summit and, join with the other U.N. Nation States, to sign these Rights into law. Yet history has proven that laws alone *do not* change conditions — *people do!*

"Do our children know about their rights?" I blurted out. "Have they had any opportunity to review them and discuss the impact of each right?"

I quickly discovered that they had *no* information about their rights — nor had children even known that they ought to be protected. By now, I felt compelled to take a more active part in this cause with the support of the San Diego Chapter of the U.N. I quickly wrote a *Ten Rights as a Child* program and met with administrators in the San Diego Unified School District. They agreed to make arrangements to get this message out to the San Diego schools.

Approximately 20 San Diego schools participated and over 25,000 letters were mailed to President Bush by the children. Still, deep inside of me, I knew that their young voices may be swallowed up in the overwhelming problems of the world. It was then that I silently vowed to make certain that young people had a collective voice, which the world would hear and acknowledge. I knew it would take a great team of human beings to stand alongside the children and give them a platform for *their* voices to be heard. With the support of *Difference Makers* around the world, the children will have that voice and stand on that platform.

Difference Makers International is committed
to providing acknowledgement trainings
for *every* child throughout the world.

**Thank you for taking a stand for our children
and making this dream come true!**

My Ten Rights as a Child

1. The right to affection, love and understanding.

2. The right to adequate nutrition and medical care.

3. The right to protection against all forms of neglect, cruelty and exploitation.

4. The right to free education and full opportunity for play and recreation.

5. The right to a name and nationality.

6. The right to special care if handicapped.

7. The right to be among the first to receive relief in times of disaster.

8. The right to learn to be useful members of society and to develop individual abilities.

9. The right to be brought up in the spirit of universal peace and brotherhood.

10. The right to enjoy these rights regardless of race, color, sex, religion, national or social origin.

Received from United Nations Association based on the 1990 World Summit for Children held at the United Nations in New York City. In appreciation for the fifty years UNICEF has worked on behalf of children's rights.

You Can Make A Difference

"Tell me the weight of a snowflake," a coal-mouse asked a wild dove.

"Nothing more than nothing," was the answer.

"In that case, I must tell you a marvelous story," the coal-mouse said.

"I sat on the branch of a fir, close to its trunk, when it began to snow — not heavily, not in a a raging blizzard — no, just like a dream, without a wound and without any violence. Since I did not have anything better to do, I counted the snowflakes settling on the twigs and needles of my branch. Their number was exactly 3,741,952. When the 3,741,953rd dropped onto the branch, nothing more than nothing, as you say — the branch broke off."

Having said that, the coal-mouse flew away.

The dove, since Noah's time an authority on the matter, thought about the story for awhile, and finally said to herself, "Perhaps there is only one person's voice lacking for peace to come to the world."

— unknown

Reprinted from: *Synchronicity*
by: Joseph Jaworski

5 Ways to Become a *Difference Maker*

1
Acknowledge Someone!

Use the Blue Ribbons included in this book to honor people in your life. Follow the instructions on the card. Know that *Who You Are Makes A Difference!*

2
Order More Books and Blue Ribbons!

Use the order form on the following page to order additional books and Blue Ribbons for your parents, children, grandparents, teachers, employees— everyone! Pass on the message!

3
Contribute Your Stories!

Many of the stories that you have read in this book were submitted by readers like you. As *Difference Makers*, we invite you too, to share a personal Blue Ribbon story or poem that you feel belongs in future volumes of *Who I Am Makes A Difference*.

So let us hear from you! Please send a copy of your stories to:

Difference Makers International
P.O. Box 2115 • Del Mar, CA 92014
FAX: (760) 634-2746 • E-Mail: blueribbon@difference-makers.com

4
Contact us for Lectures, Seminars and Workshops.

You may also contact us at the same fax and address to schedule speaking engagements for your business, organization or school, or phone us at 800-887-8422.

5
Contribute to Acknowledgement Training Programs for Children.

Each $10 tax-deductible contribution will provide the opportunity for a child to receive an acknowledgement training program, curriculum and Blue Ribbons (see contribution form at end of book).

Difference Makers
INTERNATIONAL
a non-profit educational foundation

P.O. Box 2115 • Del Mar, CA 92014 • phone: (760) 634-1851
FAX: (760) 634-2746 • E-Mail: blueribbon@difference-makers.com

Blue Ribbon Order Form

Join with other *Difference Makers* around the world...pioneers in the new millennium, weaving the language of acknowledgement into every fiber of our society, creating a sweeping change throughout our community, country and world, where dignity and respect for all people replace anger, apathy and violence.

Item	Price	S/H
Who I Am Makes a Difference Book	$14.95	$3.00

Call us for discounts on large orders.

Blue Ribbons (includes *3-Step Acknowledgement* Ceremony Cards)

Ambassador Packets	# Blue Ribbons	Price	S/H
Starter	25	$19.50	$4.00
Ambassador	50	$37.50	$5.00
Gold Ambassador	100	$67.50	$6.50
Emerald	500	$275.00	$18.75
Sapphire	1000	$500.00	$30.50

orders are available in packages up to 25,000
Blue Ribbons available in Chinese, Russian, Japanese, Spanish and Portuguese.

Call for special non-profit prices available to schools, churches and non-profit organizations.

Please photocopy this order form, fill in the information and either FAX, phone or mail in your order. CA residents please add 7.75% sales tax.

Name:

Address:

City: _____ State: _____ Zip:

Phone: _____ FAX:

Credit Card: (please circle) Visa MasterCard AMEX Discover

Credit Card Number:

Expiration Date: _____ Total: $

Signature:

To phone in order, please call 1-800-887-8422 or FAX 1-760-634-2746. California residents, call (760) 634-1851.

Difference Makers
INTERNATIONAL
a non-profit educational foundation

P.O. Box 2115 • Del Mar, CA 92014 • phone: (760) 634-1851
FAX: (760) 634-2746 • E-Mail: blueribbon@difference-makers.com

Become a Difference Maker
Contributor

"Remember a time when you were acknowledged.
What did you hear?
What did you feel?
What did you think?
What difference did it make?
Imagine that together, we can help children spread the message of acknowledgement throughout your community, country and world.
Your contribution of $10 to $10,000 makes a difference."

With love,

Helice Bridges
First Lady of Acknowledgement

Your gift will provide children the opportunity to heal relationships, connect people heart-to-heart and ignite the human spirit. Each $10 tax-deductible contribution will provide a child with acknowledgement training, Blue Ribbon curriculum and Blue Ribbons.

How many children would you like to sponsor?
I would like to sponsor _____ children @ $10.00 each.

Please photocopy this contribution form, fill in the information and either Fax, phone or mail your contribution. Thank you for making a difference!

Name: _____

Address: _____

City: _____ State: _____ Zip: _____

Phone: _____ FAX: _____

Credit Card: (please circle) Visa   MasterCard   AMEX   Discover

Credit Card Number: _____

Expiration Date: _____ Your Contribution: $ _____

Signature: _____

To contribute by phone, please call 1-800-887-8422 or FAX 1-760-634-2746.

Difference Makers
INTERNATIONAL
a non-profit educational foundation 501(c)(3)

P.O. Box 2115 • Del Mar, CA 92014 • phone: (760) 634-1851
FAX: (760) 634-2746 • E-Mail: blueribbon@difference-makers.com

THE

3-STEP BLUE RIBBON CEREMONY

Never doubt that a small group of dedicated citizens can change the world; in fact it's the only thing that ever has.
— Margaret Mead

1. **ACKNOWLEDGE SOMEONE.**
   Tell them sincerely how they make a difference to you.
2. **PLACE THE BLUE RIBBON ABOVE THEIR HEART.**
   Place the ribbon on them pointing upwards toward all their best dreams coming true. Tell them that you'll cheer them on for their dreams. Ask them to do the same for you.
3. **GIVE THEM TWO MORE RIBBONS AND TWO CEREMONY CARDS.**
   It is tradition for you to always pass on extra blue ribbons so that everyone has the opportunity to give and receive acknowledgement.

Every Blue Ribbon Ceremony you do
makes a difference.

Your words of love, support and encouragement can
change a life ***today!***

Display your Blue Ribbon as a constant reminder that
you are part of an international team of
Difference Makers

**creating a world where everyone knows
that who they are makes a difference!**

Contribute Your Stories!

Many of the stories that you have read in this book were submitted by readers like you. As *Difference Makers*, we invite you to also share a personal Blue Ribbon story or poem that you feel belongs in future volumes of *Who I Am Makes A Difference.*

So let us hear from you! Please send a copy of your stories to:

Difference Makers International
P. O. Box 2115
Del Mar CA 92014
FAX (760) 634-2746
e-mail: blueribbon@difference-makers.com

There is a story inside of us all.
Start your Blue Ribbon story here...